Business Entropy

On the emergence of order in living beings and organizations

Dr. Clemens Dachs

29.11.23

Imprint

Bibliographic information of the German National Library: The German National Library lists this publication in the German National Bibliography; detailed bibliographic data can be found on the Internet at http://dnb.dnb.de.

© 2023 Dr. Clemens Dachs

Production and published: BoD - Books on Demand, Norderstedt

ISBN: 9783758321016

Foreword

Dear reader,

In recent years, I have worked to show that organizations have a similar system dynamic and architecture to living beings. Many of nature's recipes for success can be elegantly transferred. All this is already available as a reference book or as an entertaining novel.

However, biology can only be understood more deeply if chemistry and physics are also understood. The laws of physics and chemistry apply to both animate and inanimate nature. On the one hand, every biological principle must be based on them and be explainable from them. On the other hand, you can only recognize what is special about a living being by comparing it with inanimate nature. Only then can we understand how life can rise above the inanimate world, even though it follows the same rules.

So the case is clear: if we want to have a strong foundation for the theory of bionic organization, we need to translate physics and chemistry. This will result in principles that must apply to both living and non-living organizations.

The book contains an initial thread running through physics, starting with Galileo, Newton, Boyle and Boltzmann and continuing on to chemistry.

There are certainly still many unanswered questions. But I hope that I can show in the first draft that there is a deeper insight here, and that the parallels between physics and business cannot be coincidental.

Of course, a book like this doesn't just happen on its own. I would therefore like to thank the many people who believed in me and supported me in writing it.

Special thanks go first and foremost to my family, who have supported me in my research and writing for 8 years now.

I would also like to say a special thank you to the test readers who struggled through the early versions of my ideas. Without your feedback, I would not have reached the current state.

Agnes Baumgärtner, Conny Dethloff, Michael Frahm, Martin Heider, Moritz Hornung, Wolfram Müller, Dennis Willkomm

In addition, there are many other supporters who have accompanied and inspired me in the development and publication of the ideas. Unfortunately, I can only briefly mention a few of them by name here and thank them:

Katharina Beumelburg, Christoph Fuchs, Matthias Hümmer, Hermann Kirchberger, Jürgen Kirsch, Stephan Klein, Mark Lambertz, Mona Maidorn, Martin Pfiffner, Carola Roll, Eberhard Schlücker, Simon Teeuwsen, Englbert Westermeier.

Enjoy reading,

Clemens Dachs

Dedication

For Cornelia, Felix, Regina and Valentin

Contents

1 Introduction

"Organizations simply do business as usual when there is no force acting on them."

"Organizations are inert. With large organizations, you need a lot more power to change something than with small organizations"

"You have the feeling of bouncing off the inertia of the organization if you want to change something."

"There are many forces simultaneously tugging at the organization and influencing its course."

Do you know this? Of course you do! It happens in every company. Hmmm! Of course you saw right through it. That sounds a bit like Newton's axioms. That's right! That's exactly how it is. The law of inertia, the law of motion, the law of interaction and the law of superposition.

Every body moves in a straight line if no forces act on it. The force is proportional to the acceleration, whereby the inertial mass is the proportionality factor. Force is equal to counterforce. Forces are superimposed.

Newton knew that. And you already know that from physics and presumably from your company.

You may now be asking yourself, "Why should we translate the principles of physics and chemistry into the world of organizations? What's in it for me?"

The reason for this is that organizations are living systems. Of course, you can also use well-known methods from other companies as a guide. When it comes to growth, living beings are far superior to organizations. A bacterium doubles in size every 30 minutes, 100 trillion cells work together in the human body, without any chief cell. This is described in detail in the books Viable Project Business, Cell Culture and Autopoiesis. Many principles of biology can be transferred to organizations. And biology is based on chemistry and physics. This book translates these principles.

On the journey, we will then get to know the analogies to important concepts. What is mass, momentum, energy, internal energy, temperature, and - the most colorful term of all - entropy?

Let's go back to biology again. The cell is our model and we want to understand exactly which system dynamics enable it to achieve high growth rates. Let's take a look at two of the principles that have already been described in detail in the other books.

In the cell, every chemical reaction is accelerated by enzymes. These enzymes do not exist by chance, but because the cell builds them itself. This is a central feedback loop: autocatalysis. A living system builds catalysts to accelerate every single process. In an organization, this corresponds to the best working conditions for all processes. But how often do you have that? Rarely. That's why you can look in biology books to see how a simple bacterium manages to accelerate every single chemical reaction to such an extent.

Another mechanism of cells is based on concentration. Cells pump nutrients in and waste out so that they always have the highest concentration. In an organization, too, you have to try to create the highest concentration of success factors. Many agile methods try to increase concentration. Here, too, you realize that everything is based on sophisticated system dynamics and architecture.

Of course, there is much more to transfer. But let's stick with these two examples. Both mechanisms of biology are based on properties of chemistry, which in turn are based on physics.

The catalysis with which the cell works is a chemical phenomenon. Catalysts reduce the free energy required for a reaction. But what is free energy? What is energy in this context? And what are concentration gradients and diffusion? How does a system manage to increase the concentration?

The question about both phenomena is: Why does a cell manage to create order at all, even though all molecules do what they want. Molecules do not know that they are in a cell and have a task. Newton has just explained to us that such a particle only obeys the laws of nature. So how can something as complex as life exist?

This is also the question in organizations: If everyone in our company does what they want, why can the company grow?

The book aims to answer all these questions.

You may be asking yourself: "Why is that even possible to translate? I'm sure it will be a nice metaphor, but how valid is it?"

And they are absolutely right to be critical. But we have a powerful ally on our journey: Mathematics! Many findings in physics are mathematical conclusions from Newton's axioms. For example, the law of conservation of energy follows directly from Newton's law of motion $F = m \cdot a$ for purely mathematical reasons. Anyone who says yes to Newton must also say yes to the conservation of energy. Anyone who says yes to kinetic energy must also say yes to internal energy. Entropy is a purely mathematical concept anyway. We follow this mathematical trail right through physics.

Despite all my enthusiasm for the topic, I still have to go back to your question: How stable is it all? It is as good as I was able to write it in the first version. There are certainly a lot of unanswered questions and doubts. So if you have any further questions, or even ideas for solving the problems, I would be very happy to receive your feedback. Then the next edition will be much stronger with your help.

Have fun reading through and gaining new insights.

And off we go ...

2 Location and speed

The physicist Lord Kelvin is credited with the statement: "You can't improve what you can't measure." This applies not only to physics, but also to organizations. Edward Deming, the father of quality management, also applied the idea to management. He also coined the saying "In God we trust, all others bring data".

Why are figures, data and facts so important? They provide a good basis for decisions. Of course, some important factors cannot be measured. Nevertheless, decisions are often better if they are made in the knowledge of facts.

Imagine you want to bring about change in your organization. You create new tools, work on product modularization and change processes. All of this has a purpose: the organization should be more successful afterwards than before. But how can you assess whether you have achieved your goal? To do this, you need to know where the organization was yesterday, where it is today and where it wants to go.

This is precisely the task of key figures. Key figures try to express in numbers where the organization stands. Improvements to the processes should lead to an improvement in the key figures. The change in products and processes is a cause that has the measurable effect of improving the key figures.

Exactly this relationship between cause and effect can also be found in the classical mechanics of Galileo and Newton.

2.1 Place and speed in physics

So let's start at the very beginning of modern science - with classical mechanics.

Kinematics explains what acceleration in space is. To this end, it examines time, location, speed, direction and acceleration in three-dimensional space. All of this is strongly based on the geometry of space.

Dynamics examines the different types of forces that act on point masses and accelerate them. Newton's axioms establish a connection between force as a cause and acceleration as an effect.

Kinematics and dynamics can therefore be used to predict the movement of particles in the presence of forces. The movement of the particles makes the causative forces observable.

The special thing about classical mechanics is its strict mathematization. Only very few physical observations are assumed as axioms; everything else is then derived strictly mathematically. If these axioms are true, the conclusions must also be correct.

This also helps when transferring the concepts to the world of organizations. If there is a plausible translation of space and time, then derived quantities such as distance, speed and acceleration can be translated purely mathematically. They are then also necessarily valid. This is precisely the strength of the axiomatic method of mathematics. It is based on axioms that are assumed to be true but cannot be proven. All conclusions then result purely from the logic of mathematics.

Let's take a closer look at the kinematics.

Space and time

Space and time are probably the most fundamental concepts in all of physics. All other concepts such as force and energy later build on them. Classical mechanics uses the non-curved three-dimensional Euclidean space, in which there is a uniform time. Today we know that this is only a simplification that does not apply to large speeds, masses or even the smallest objects. For our purposes, however, it is a good starting point.

What is a location in space? It can be said that a particle A is located at a time t_1 at the location coordinates (x, y, z). These location coordinates are properties of particle A at a certain point in time.

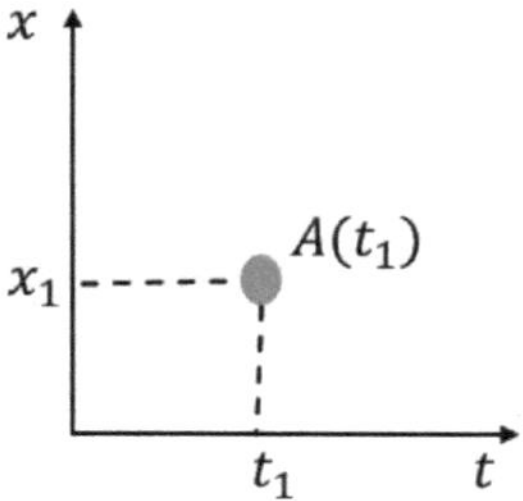

Figure 1: An object A has the x-location coordinate x1 at time t1.

There is a special feature here: If the particle AB consists of several sub-particles A and B, then the composite particle AB has the same location as the sub-particles A and B (more precisely: it is located at the center of gravity of the system). For this reason, an atom is also located where the nucleus and the electrons are, and a molecule is located where the individual atoms are.

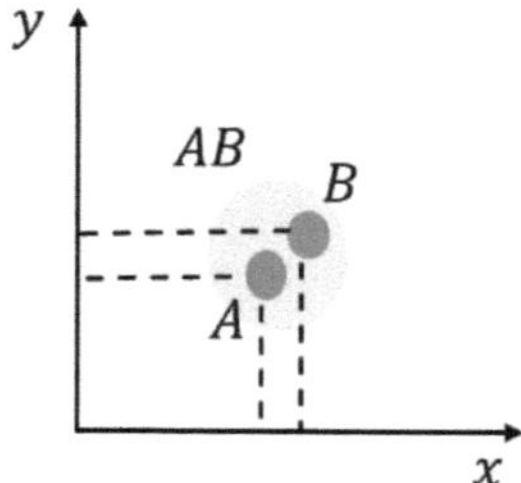

Figure 2: The composite object AB consists of the parts A and B, each of which has an x and y coordinate. The location of AB corresponds to the center of gravity of the locations of A and B.

We will discuss the concept of the center of gravity of composite objects in more detail later.

Speed

It is easy to move from the concept of location to the concept of speed. The velocity v describes the distance a particle travels in a certain period of time.

The **average speed** is the quotient of the location difference and the time difference, i.e. $v = \frac{\Delta x}{\Delta t} = (x_2 - x_1)/(t_2 - t_1)$.

If you shorten the time span more and more up to the limiting case $dt = 0$ the **instantaneous velocity** is obtained. The following applies $v = ds\,/\,dt$ therefore the first derivative is formed. Just like the location, the velocity is a vector and therefore has a direction and a magnitude.

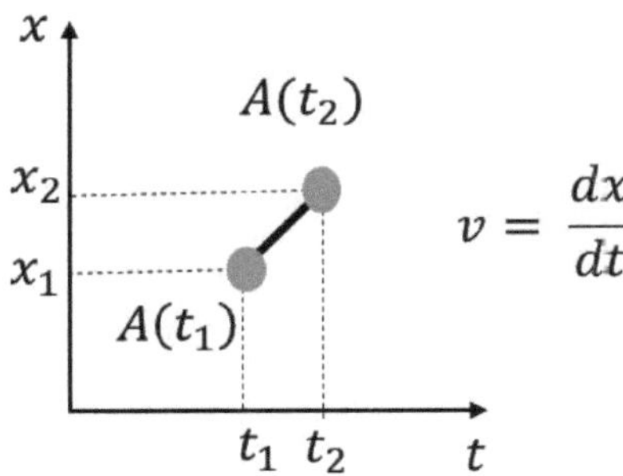

Figure 3: An object A has the location coordinate x1 at time t1 and the location coordinate x2 at time t2. The speed is the distance in space divided by the time required.

Acceleration

Acceleration is defined as the change in velocity over time, i.e. $a = dv/dt$. Both the amount and the direction of the velocity can change.

In the simple case of acceleration $a = 0$ we speak of a rectilinear, uniform movement. Linear means that the direction is not changed. Uniform means that the amount of speed is not changed.

One of Galileo Galilei's great achievements was to clearly define the difference between velocity and acceleration. In everyday life, there are no straight, uniform movements, because various forces such as gravity and friction always change the velocity. However, it was only by formulating constant velocity as a reference point that acceleration and forces could be investigated in more detail.

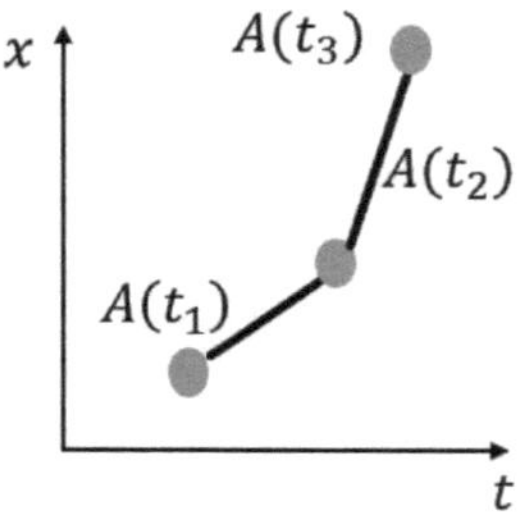

Figure 4: An object A is moving. The speed between t2 and t3 is higher than between t1 and t2. The object is therefore accelerated.

The aforementioned concepts of location, velocity and acceleration are therefore related by derivatives and each represent vectors in three-dimensional space.

2.2   The location and velocity of the organization

Key figures as a positioning tool for organizations

Where is an organization located? What are its coordinates at a certain point in time? Every organization can be characterized by key figures. If there are n key figures for an organization, it can be described by n values. The location of an organization is therefore the point in the n-dimensional key figure space. It can be specified as an n-vector.

Since there are any number of key figures, every organization has a different place in practice. No two organizations or teams are absolutely identical in all conceivable key figures.

What types of key figures are we talking about?

Key figure principle 1: Key figures for localization refer to a point in time, not a period of time.

If key figures are used to locate an organization in a key figure space, the key figures must relate to a point in time, not a period of time.

Turnover and profit are therefore not suitable as location coordinates because they are properties of a time period (such as a year) and not of a point in time.

Key figure principle 2: Key figures for localization must be relative values.

Secondly, they must be ratios. This is because the location of an organization with two departments should lie between the locations of the departments. This is not true for absolute values.

Equity is therefore not suitable because the values of two companies included in a group would add up and not result in an average value. The group would have a completely different location than the companies it contains.

Relative key figures that relate to a point in time (e.g. a reporting date) are therefore more suitable.

- Equity / number of employees
- Equity / share
- Equity / total capital
- Proportion of disabled persons / number of employees

Evaluations such as satisfaction are also possible, as composite organizations always work with the average instead of the total.

- Average employee satisfaction (because an average is calculated from quantitative evaluations)
- Average customer satisfaction.

The location of an organization therefore corresponds to the vector of its relative key figures.

Velocity of organizations

The velocity in the key figure space corresponds to the rate of change of a key figure.

Key figure principle 3: Key figures that relate to a period of time are velocities.

Key figures that refer to a time period must always include the time period (such as profit/employee/year). They are comparable to an average velocity. If an instantaneous velocity can be calculated from this by reducing the time period, the instantaneous velocity is obtained.

An example of a key figure is $X = E/H =$ Equity/headcount. Let us assume that the headcount H is constant. If we compare the key figure at the end with the beginning of the year, the difference is $dX = d(E/H) = dE/H =$ profit/employee. The speed in this coordinate is therefore $dX/dt =$ the profit per employee per year.

It becomes somewhat more difficult if the denominator of the key figure changes. In this example, the number of employees could have doubled, but the equity is constant. Or both values change. Even if the derivative is then determined using the quotient rule, the value of the speed is still easy to calculate.

If the velocity is constant, the future values could now be extrapolated. From the value at the time (t_0), the velocity and the duration t, the equity/headcount at any time t could be determined.

The situation is similar with all other key figures. At constant velocity, the organization moves in a straight line through the key figure space. This can often be seen in diagrams in which a variable is extrapolated linearly. Of course, there is no organization where this is true. The speeds are constantly changing and are also different for each coordinate. Obviously, there is also an acceleration.

Acceleration of the organization

This brings us to a central concept of management: **change**. Change is a change in the linear, uniform course of the organization. **Change in key figures is synonymous with acceleration.** Change can therefore be observed through a non-linear change in key figures. Both the amount of speed and the direction of the organization can be changed.

In this book, we therefore do not look at change from a psychological perspective, but purely from the measurable effect in the key figures.

How do you calculate the acceleration? Let's take the last example again. The velocity with respect to the coordinate X = E / H was dX/dt = profit/employee/year. Now this value can change from one year to the next, it can increase or decrease. The acceleration is the difference between the velocities divided by the duration, i.e. per year.

How can this be interpreted? An acceleration of 0 indicates that the organization is developing linearly. A high acceleration indicates that the organization is developing significantly differently than if the straight-line course had been extrapolated.

If there is different acceleration in the various key figures, this corresponds to a change of direction in space. The organization is changing course.

2.3 Findings

What does the translation of kinematics provide us with? Kinematics investigates the movements of particles in space. Dynamics later explains why these particles move.

We view the organization as an object in an n-dimensional key figure space. With its current values, it has a unique location that can change over time.

As in physics, for various reasons there are no organizations that change in a straight line and uniformly. However, in order to be able to investigate the reasons for the course changes, it is important to understand this special case of constant speed as a reference point. Only then can acceleration be measured and the reasons for the change can be investigated.

Why is all this so important? Let's compare physics again. Forces can only be recognized through their effects on particles. This is what makes forces measurable. Even time can only be measured through movement in space.

It is the same in organizations. All forces in the organization cause key figures to change. Studying the characteristics of key figures is therefore a prerequisite before you can turn to the much more important question: What exactly causes key figures to change? But for this we need to look at the dynamics.

3 Mass

In the last chapter, we saw that organizations can be located using key figures. Organizations move in the key figure space and have a certain velocity. This velocity can change in size and direction over time.

In this chapter, we want to examine this in more detail. What is the cause of the change in motion? Sir Issac Newton answered precisely this question for physics in detail in 1686 in his work Philosophiae Naturalis Principia Mathematica.

3.1 Newton's laws

While kinematics investigates the nature of movements, dynamics is concerned with their causes. The question is: What causes a point mass to change its current course?

The central concepts here are the inertial system, force, inertial mass and momentum. These concepts are introduced in Newton's laws. It turns out that there are a small number of basic forces that overlap and lead to the acceleration of a point mass.

What can we hope for in terms of understanding organizations? We have learned from kinematics that organizations have a location in the key figure space and move there. Of course, we want our organization to have good key figures, i.e. to develop in a certain direction. Translating the dynamics can now provide new insights into how the organization can move towards success.

Newton's axioms

Newton's four laws are axioms. They are based on empirical observations of nature and are formulated as mathematical statements. Building on this, further work can be carried out using mathematical means. Mathematically substantiated conclusions from the axioms can then be verified empirically.

The four laws are as follows:

1. A body remains at rest or in rectilinear, uniform motion if no force acts on it. $F = 0 \implies a = 0$
2. The acceleration of a body is proportional to the force acting on it. $F = m \cdot a$
3. For every force there is an opposing force of the same magnitude and in the opposite direction. $F_{12} = -F_{21}$
4. A linear combination of forces leads to a linear combination of accelerations.

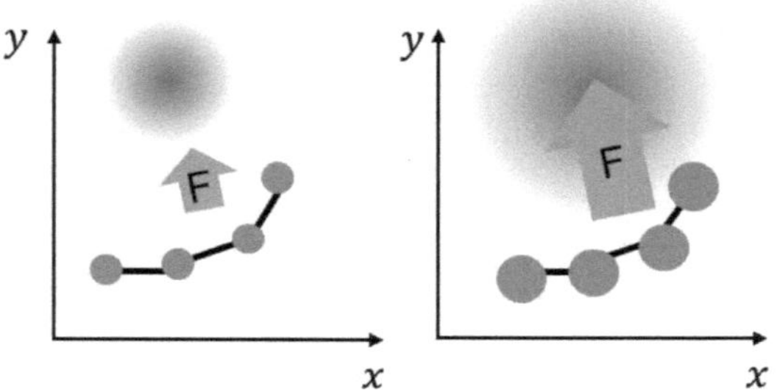

Figure 5: Left: An object with little mass needs a small force to experience a certain acceleration. Right: If the mass is higher, a greater force is required.

The four laws link the change in linear, uniform motion with a force. This means that not only the cause can be related to an effect. The relationship also makes it possible to quantify forces by measuring the resulting acceleration.

Let's take a closer look at the individual laws.

Law of inertia

Newton's first law is the law of inertia.

A body remains at rest or in linear, uniform motion if no force acts on it.

$$F = 0 \implies a = 0$$

This relationship links force as a cause with acceleration as an effect. Without force, there is no acceleration.

If the acceleration is zero, this means that the speed should not change. This always requires a reference point of observation, the **inertial frame of reference**. An **inertial frame** is a reference point from which particles on which no force acts move in a straight line and uniformly. It can be shown that, if such an inertial frame exists at all, then any reference point that is displaced, rotated or moving at a constant speed is also an inertial frame.

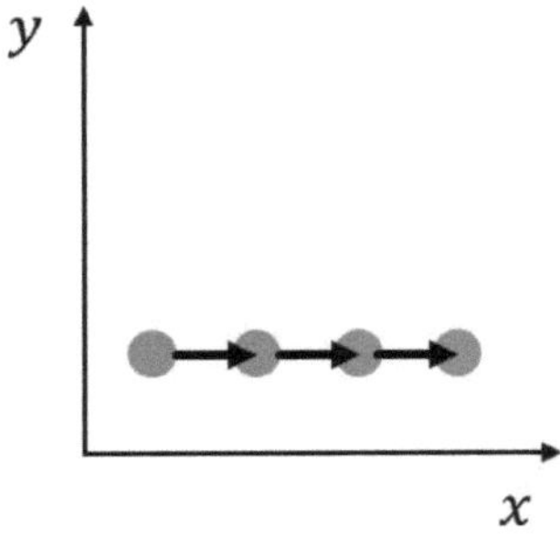

Figure 6: A particle moves in a straight line and uniformly when no force is applied.

Law of motion

Newton's second law is the law of motion.

The acceleration a of a body is proportional to the force acting on it F. The **inertial mass** m of a body is the proportionality factor.

$$F = m \cdot a$$

As in Newton's first law, a force is the cause of acceleration. However, there is now the inertial mass as a factor.

The inertial mass m is therefore a scalar property of a body that indicates how much the body resists acceleration. The greater the inertial mass, the less acceleration is achieved with the same force.

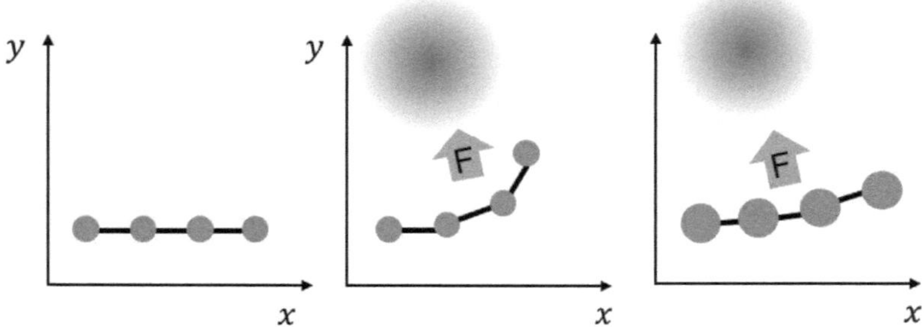

Figure 7: The higher the inertia, the lower the acceleration with the same force.

Law of interaction

Newton's third law is the law of interaction. It is better known as "Actio = Reactio".

Each force is countered by an equal counterforce.

$$F_{21} = -F_{12}$$

When a body exerts a force on another body, it always experiences a force of the same magnitude but in the opposite direction.

The law of interaction generally applies to all types of forces. This means that there are no bodies that are pure causers of forces on others, or vice versa. The same force always acts back. Only the mass of a body determines how strongly it is accelerated.

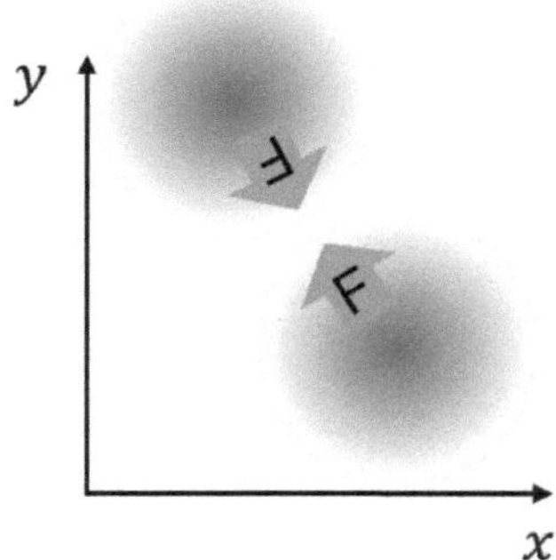

Figure 8: Each force is countered by a counterforce of the same magnitude and in the opposite direction.

Law of superposition

The last law is the law of superposition, also known as the superposition principle.

A sum of forces leads to a sum of accelerations.

$$F = F_1 + F_2 = m \cdot (a_1 + a_2) = m \cdot a$$

Both forces and accelerations are vectors. They are therefore always added component by component. Graphically, the addition of forces can be represented as a force parallelogram, whereby the resulting force is always the diagonal of the parallelogram.

As every body in the universe has a mass and therefore exerts a gravitational force on other bodies, the forces of all these bodies overlap and then generate a resulting force that acts on one body. This means that practically an infinite number of forces are superimposed at every point in the universe. Conversely, each body also influences the entire universe.

Newton's first theorem therefore refers to the resulting force, which is the superposition of the forces of all bodies at a point. This can be zero, even if the individual contributions to the sum are not equal to zero.

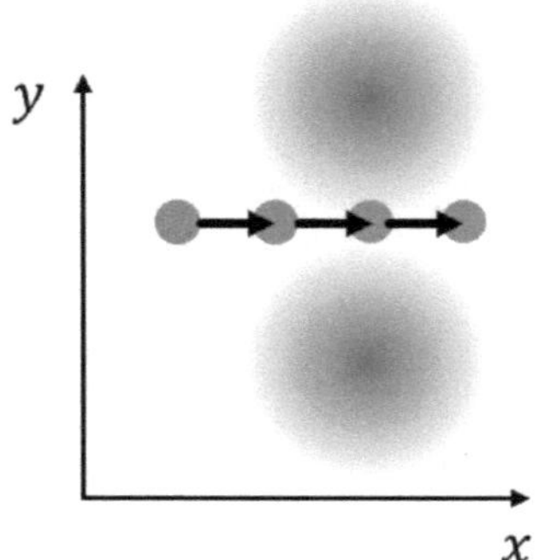

Figure 9: Forces are superimposed at every point in space to form a resultant force.

Forces

We now know that particles are accelerated by forces. But where do the forces come from? The particles are not only accelerated by forces. They are also the cause of such forces themselves.

One example of this is the force of gravity. Every mass m_1 leads to an attractive force on other masses m_2. The following applies:

$$F = G \cdot m_1 m_2 / r^2$$

Here G is the gravitational constant and r is the distance. You can also see the symmetry in the equation. The force acts on both masses in different directions.

Another example is the Coulomb force of the electric charge. Every charge q_1 leads to an attractive or repulsive force on other charges q_2.

$$F = \frac{\varepsilon}{2\pi} * q_1 q_2 / r^2$$

Here ε is the dielectric constant of the medium and r is the distance between the charges.

In contrast to the gravitational force, the Coulomb force does not act on all particles, but only on charged particles. However, a neutron has no charge. It is therefore neither the source of a Coulomb force, nor can it be accelerated by others through this force. In contrast to gravity, the Coulomb force has both an attractive and a repulsive effect.

Otherwise, however, these forces overlap at every point and lead to acceleration there.

Momentum

Newton's law of motion $F = m \cdot a$ leads us to a new concept: momentum is a property of a body that is calculated as the product of mass and velocity.

$$p = m \cdot v$$

This quantity has the property that it is additive. If two bodies with masses m_1 and m_2 and the same velocity v have the impulses p_1 and p_2 the impulses add up.

$$p = m \cdot v = m_1 \cdot v + m_2 \cdot v = p_1 + p_2$$

Newton's law of motion can also be written with the momentum $F = m \cdot a$ can also be written as

$$F = \dot{p} = dp(t)/dt$$

If there is no external force, the momentum of a body is conserved. This is exactly what the law of conservation of momentum states. Momentum is therefore a property that characterizes a body. Bodies with a high mass have a higher momentum at the same speed than bodies with a low mass.

3.2   The inertia of the organization

A first overview

How can Newton's concepts be applied to organizations?

Newton's axioms apply to organizations:

1. Organizations remain on their current course if no force is exerted on them.
2. The change in an organization's course is proportional to this force. Proportionality corresponds to the inertia of the organization.
3. For every force there is an opposing force. The originator of a change feels a force himself.
4. The various forces acting on a company overlap and add up vectorially.

Let's take a closer look at these statements.

The persistence of organizations on their course

Newton's first law for organizations is:

Organizations remain on their course if no forces act on them.

This is precisely the purpose of change management. Change management aims to change organizations - measurably. Continuing the status quo on the current course is not change. Change means that the direction or amount of speed changes. If no forces are at work, nothing changes.

The cause and effect of change

Now, every organization will react differently to these forces. This corresponds precisely to the inertia of the organization, i.e. its inert mass. Small organizations can often change faster than large ones. They have less inertial mass, which keeps them on a constant course.

This can be seen in change management. People are creatures of habit and often stick to their course. Changing the course of a single person requires strength. In departments with many people, the forces add up.

As a very first approximation, let us assume that a group of n average people are n times more difficult to change than a single average person. One could ascribe to each person an inertia against change.

Of course, there are often very complex group dynamics that have not yet been taken into account. However, it helps to look at the people to be changed individually. Based on this, you can then examine the effects of group dynamics in more detail. This is analogous to constant velocity, which does not really exist, but is an excellent reference point for measuring acceleration.

Interactions

People and organizations are not only inert and resistant to change. They are also the cause of this change.

Organizations are changed by forces. But these forces always have an originator. These can be people who fill a role, such as the CEO. Or it can be other organizations, such as a competitor.

If the new CEO advocates a certain idea or approach, then he wants the organization to move in a certain direction. However, the organization also changes the CEO in the process. He has to make compromises and move towards the organization. Forces therefore affect the organization and the CEO in equal measure. Who moves more is a question of inertia, or to put it more positively: steadfastness.

The same applies to two organizations that have products for the same target group. One organization pushes the other out of the market. The loser has to change course. But a force has also been exerted on the winner.

The superposition of many forces

Many forces also act simultaneously in organizations. These overlap and then form a resultant force at each point.

In this way, all employees and all investors, customers and suppliers have an impact on an organization. The various forces add up. Depending on whether they point in the same direction or not, they either reinforce each other or cancel each other out.

In the end, this resulting force causes an organization to change course.

Forces in the organization

Every organization and all employees are influenced by forces. But the reverse is also true: every employee is the source of many forces and thus changes other people or the entire organization.

The forces can vary in strength. They also only affect other people who are receptive to them (i.e. who couple to the field). They can have an attractive or repulsive effect.

One example is the role model function of managers. Setting an example of good qualities or high productivity has the effect that others also want to acquire these qualities and change their course.

Influence and power also play a role. By setting targets, a CEO causes all departments to change direction. Of course, he is also influenced in turn by the employees.

The momentum

Now the inertia of an organization should not be seen as a pure problem. Momentum is mass times speed. An inertial organization that is moving in the right direction will stay on course even if it doesn't do anything. It has high momentum. It is precisely the employees who are seen as inflexible who ensure that the organization continues to run and is not completely thrown off balance by the slightest disruption. However, a high level of inertia also requires a great deal of strength for change.

The calculation of mass in organizations

In contrast to 3-dimensional physical space, our ratio space is not isotropic. The key figures have different meanings. For this reason, mass as inertia must always be seen in relation to a specific index. It is also a vector here, just like momentum and force, and must therefore be considered separately for each spatial direction.

The question is always: Which factors counteract the change in a certain key figure?

Let's concentrate on a simple interpretation:

Large organizations are more difficult to change than small ones. Let's relate the size to the number of employees. Many people have to be influenced to bring about change.

Of course, every single employee is different. Some change more easily, others more severely. If you look at many employees, there is an average value. We can calibrate this: The average person has an inertia value of 1. Each person can then have a different value relative to this, and have higher or lower values.

If we again consider a very large number of people, then the total inertia corresponds to the sum of the employees, because the deviations from the average value 1 are averaged out. The following therefore applies:

Mass = number of employees

Of course, there are other factors of inertia, such as inflexible software tools or complex decision-making processes. These also work against change. The greater the inertia, the less change with the same force.

If you have already read Autopoiesis, you will recognize where this is going. A living system like a cell is an autocatalyst and essentially consists of catalysts and the molecules from which something is built. An organization is also an autocatalyst and therefore consists of the factors to produce the production capacity. In the lean world, this is called people, machines, materials, methods, management and the environment. These factors and their precise interaction are the components of the organization. At the same time, they represent its inertia. Each of the factors, and all of them in combination, work against change.

For the moment, however, let's stick with the very simple interpretation of inertia as the number of employees.

The calculation of momentum and force in organizations

On this basis, we can now also interpret the momentum and the force, because it applies:

Momentum = mass * velocity

Force = mass * acceleration = change in momentum.

How does this look in concrete examples?

Example 1:

We start again with the equity and formulate a location coordinate.

Location x	Equity / Employees
Distance dx	Profit / employees
Speed v = dx / dt	Profit / Employees / Time
Mass m	Number of employees
Momentum p = m * v	Profit / time
Force F = dp/dt	Change in profit/time per time

Example 2:

This can also be used in a similar way in production. We look at the absolute number of products manufactured. This is not the number per unit of time, but the total number of all items ever produced since the company was founded or a certain cut-off date. The reference point is therefore relative and can be set arbitrarily. The output quantity is the quantity of new products added.

Location x	Total products manufactured / employees
Distance	Newly produced products / employees

dx	= Product quantity / employee
Velocity v=dx/dt	Output quantity / employees / time = Labor productivity
Mass m	Number of employees
Momentum p = m*v	Output quantity / time = Output
Force F = dp/dt	Momentum change = change in output per time

This parameter results in labor productivity as the speed and output (=output/time) as the impulse.

Here you can also clearly see the relationship between the spatial coordinate and the momentum. If the original parameter was calculated per person, then the momentum is the change in the parameter per time. The principle always applies if the inertia is in the denominator of the spatial coordinate. When calculating the momentum, the inertia is removed again.

If, for example, the total resource costs rather than the number of employees had been used in the inertia and location coordinates, the speed would be the total factor productivity, but the momentum would still be the output.

Despite this similarity to existing key figures, there is one key difference. Here, the number of employees is viewed as inertia, and not in terms of costs. The focus is not on productivity, but on the fact that something resists change and stays on course. In both cases, however, it is a question of evaluating the factors of production. In the classic models according to costs, and here according to resistance to change.

3.3 Findings

Since organizations have their own complex system dynamics, it is difficult to accept this connection. However, this was similar in early physics. Linear, uniform motion is not found in everyday life, as friction and gravity always have an effect. Physics would have an even harder time if the laws had been tested immediately on living beings. A hamster falls down, a bird obviously does not. It is also difficult to determine the inertia of a horse. You can push it twice with one force and nothing happens. Suddenly it starts running on its own. Despite all this, Newton's laws also apply to hamsters, birds and horses. They all have an inertial mass and obey the laws of physics. As living beings, however, they also have their own complex dynamics, which are nevertheless based on physics. These dynamics can only be described if they are compared with the inanimate normal case.

It is the same with organizations. If an organization has business as usual in its purest form and proceeds in exactly the same way, then it will always have the same results. The key figures that accumulate then result in a linear variable that is dependent on time. Any deviation from strict business as usual is seen here as the result of a changing force.

Newton's axioms introduced the concepts of inertial mass and force to physics. Particles move in a straight line and uniformly if no force is applied. However, if a force is acting, the acceleration is proportional to the force. The inertial mass is the proportionality factor.

Newton's axioms now apply to organizations:

1. Organizations remain on their current course if no force acts on them. Their key figures for time periods (e.g.: profit/employee/year) are constant.
2. The change in an organization's course is proportional to this force. Proportionality corresponds to the inertia of the organization.
3. For every force, there is an opposing force that acts on the causer in the opposite direction.
4. The various forces acting on an organization overlap and add up vectorially.

The term mass obviously describes the opposite of agility. While agility involves reacting quickly and adapting your own course, mass describes a measure of inertia.

So you could say that agile companies try to have a low inertial mass so that they can make a quick course correction with little force. This is certainly helpful or even necessary in some situations, but in others inertia also has a high value.

The momentum links the velocity with the inertia in the same way. A high momentum indicates that a high speed could be achieved despite inertia and that this speed can be maintained even if there are disturbances.

4 Energy

Organizations therefore have an impulse that keeps them on course. They change this course when forces act on them. The inertia of the organization determines how much force is required to change the key figures.

Now you can also ask yourself how much change has already been accumulated in an organization. How many forces has it already been exposed to in order to arrive at the current key figures? In other words, it is about the change work that has already been carried out, which has made the organization what it is.

Since organizations and employees are also the creators of forces, we can ask ourselves what overall change they are capable of.

It is precisely these questions that lead us to the concept of energy in organizations. What can we learn from physics?

4.1 Energy in physics

Energy is one of the central quantities in physics. All of thermodynamics and modern chemistry are based on it.

Despite this significance, it took a long time for the concept of energy and the law of conservation of energy to be discovered. In Newton's time, it did not yet play a major role. The reason may well be that energy was even further distanced from the observable quantities of space and time than the force. Energy played just as little a role in the observation of the planets as it did with energy sources on earth such as wind or water power. This changed with the invention of the steam engine and the emergence of thermodynamics. Using coal as a fuel for steam engines, it quickly became clear that a measure of stored work was needed that would ultimately exert a force on a piston. Over time, the phenomenon became better and better understood. Today, everyone is familiar with energy in kilowatt hours, even if this quantity cannot be experienced directly, but only indirectly through its effects.

The definition of energy and the law of conservation of energy

The conservation of energy is a direct mathematical consequence of Newton's equation of motion $F = m \cdot a$. The thought process is not very difficult, and so beautiful, so I will briefly explain it here.

$$0 = m \cdot a - F$$

We will transform this equation several times. First, we multiply both sides by v.

$$0 = m \cdot a \cdot v - F \cdot v.$$

We integrate both sides over time.

$$\int 0 \, dt = \int mav \, dt - \int Fv \, dt$$

Now we transform the integrals by substitution so that the first summand becomes the integral of the speed and the second the integral of the location.

$$\int 0 \, dt = \int m \frac{dv}{dt} v \, dt - \int F \frac{dx}{dt} \, dt$$

$$\int 0 \, dt = \int mv \, dv - \int F \, dx$$

The first two integrals are easy to solve.

$$E_0 = \frac{1}{2} mv^2 + E_1 - \int F \, dx$$

If the integration constants are combined, the result is the energy E which is made up of two summands.

$$E = E_0 - E_1 = \frac{1}{2} mv^2 - \int F \, dx$$

The first summand is the **kinetic energy**

$$E_{kin}(v) = \frac{1}{2} m \cdot v^2 \,.$$

The second summand is the **potential energy**, which only depends on the location.

$$E_{pot}(x) = -\int_0^x F(x)dx$$

The **law of conservation of energy** is obtained

$$E = E_{kin} + E_{pot} = const.$$

The sum of kinetic and potential energy is constant.

The importance of energy and the law of conservation of energy

The total energy of a single point mass therefore consists of two parts. One part of the energy, the kinetic energy, depends only on the speed of the particle. The other part, the potential energy, depends only on its location. If no energy is added or released, the energy is constant. In this case, however, potential energy can be converted into kinetic energy - or vice versa.

A simple example is a ball rolling up a hill. It has a speed, i.e. kinetic energy. As it rolls uphill, the ball gains altitude energy until its speed is zero at the highest point. All the energy has been converted from kinetic to potential energy. When rolling downhill, the potential energy is converted back into kinetic energy.

We will refine this later and also look at the case of friction, in which energy appears to disappear. This energy reappears as internal energy, becomes noticeable as temperature, and forms the central variable of thermodynamics. But more on this later. Let's transfer the concept of energy.

4.2   The energy of the organization

You were probably already familiar with the terms relating to energy from school. However, the mathematical derivation from the law of motion was important to me for a particular reason:

Anyone who says yes to Newton's laws must also say yes to the conservation of energy. The law of conservation of energy is a direct mathematical consequence of the equation of motion. The sum of kinetic and potential energy is constant for point masses.

In physics, too, the concept of energy was anything but intuitive at first. Nevertheless, it later emerged as a central variable. Let's take the same approach with organizations.

Potential energy of the organization

The potential energy corresponds to the sum of the forces that had to be overcome on the way from the starting point to the current location. You gain potential energy, just like a mountain climber who gains altitude energy.

In the case of an organization, the location is indicated by key figures. If the status of the key figures at an earlier point in time is selected as the reference point of the journey (inertial system), then the potential energy corresponds to the sum of all efforts to achieve the current status of the location key figures.

$$E_{pot}(x) = -\int_0^x F(x)dx$$

Kinetic energy of the organization

High kinetic energy corresponds to the fact that an organization that is actually inert now moves at high speed. Precisely because it is so inert, it had to be accelerated with a lot of force in order to reach this high speed. Due to the conservation of momentum, this high speed is maintained even if no other forces are applied.

$$E_{kin} = \frac{1}{2}m \cdot v^2$$

What does this value mean? It consists of the speed ratios, squared, and the inertia to be overcome. Because of the square, it does not matter in which direction the key figures change. The more they change, the higher the energy, regardless of whether they improve or deteriorate. The energy only expresses how strong the change is, not the direction.

The total energy

As in physics, energy now consists of two summands:

The first summand, the kinetic energy, describes a measure of the effort required to arrive at the current velocity figures.

The second summand, the potential energy, describes the sum of the forces acting in order to get from a starting point to the current location parameters.

The law of conservation of energy now follows from Newton's law of motion. If no other forces are acting and no energy is lost dissipatively (through friction), the sum of the two energies remains the same.

This law of conservation of energy cannot be observed in real organizations. Why is that, if the theorem follows mathematically from the axioms?

This is because real organizations are not dead systems that drift, but are alive and therefore constantly feed in energy from outside. On the other hand, they also constantly lose energy through internal friction. They are therefore not isolated.

Even if we do not observe this theoretical, isolated case, we can still consider the two components of energy and formulate the generalization that the sum of these forms of energy is constant if there were no changes due to energy inflows or outflows. We will examine these energy inflows and outflows in detail later.

Perhaps they have once again recognized the idealization that is also repeatedly found in physics. We have already seen this with linear motion, which does not exist anywhere in the universe. The ideal cases do not serve to ignore reality, but as a point of reference in order to be able to examine the deviations more closely.

The calculation of the energy

The kinetic energy can be calculated very simply from the previous values. The potential energy is not listed here because it results from the environment of the organization.

We continue with the calculations from the last chapter.

Example 1:

Location x	Equity / Employees
Distance dx	Profit / employees
Speed v = dx / dt	Profit / Employees / Time
Mass M	Number of employees
Kinetic energy $E_{kin} = mv^2$	½ * employee * (profit/employee/time)² = ½ * (profit/time)² / employee

Example 2:

Location x	Total products manufactured / employees
Distance dx	Newly produced products / employees = output quantity / employee
Velocity v=dx/dt	Output quantity / employees / time = Labor productivity
Mass m	Number of employees
Kinetic energy $E_{kin} = mv^2$	½ * Employees * (output quantity/employee/time)² = ½ * Output² / employee

Both examples show that kinetic energy leads to non-intuitive key figures that have a quadratic factor. This square factor comes from the velocity.

4.3 Findings

We have now become familiar with energy as a central concept. While the previous concepts such as force, momentum and acceleration always act at a specific point in time, with energy these variables are added up over a period of time.

In the case of organizations, energy therefore expresses the efforts that were necessary in the past to bring the organization to where it is today.

The kinetic energy describes the effort required to achieve the current speed, i.e. the key figures of the change. The potential energy describes the sum of the forces required to achieve the current inventory figures.

Since an organization is in constant exchange with the environment, gaining or releasing energy in the process, no law of conservation of energy will be observed. Furthermore, an organization is not a monolithic point mass, but is composed of parts. We will see in a moment that energy seems to be lost in such composite systems and is found again in internal energy. Let's take a closer look at this effect.

5 Internal energy

Now that we have established the basics, we can turn our attention to systems. We want to shed light on how the properties of the components relate to the properties of the overall system.

Why is this important for organizations? Organizations consist of business units, departments, and these in turn consist of teams and roles. We want to create a bridge between the characteristics of the roles and the characteristics of the organization as a whole. In particular, we are interested in how the key figures of the parts relate to the key figures of the organization as a whole.

We also established in the last chapter that the law of conservation of energy does not seem to apply to organizations. We will now examine one of the reasons in more detail. The energy of organizations is not lost, but is converted into internal energy and is no longer visible in the key figures.

This phenomenon is typical for nested systems. Let's take a look at this using physics.

5.1 Internal energy in physics

It has long been known in physics that energy appears to be lost. If I roll a ball along a straight track, it will eventually come to a standstill. However, the kinetic energy has not been lost, but has been converted into another form of energy, the internal energy, through friction. This form of energy is now perceptible through an increase in temperature. What happens in detail?

Multi-particle systems and center of gravity

We now move from the single point mass to a multi-particle system consisting of n particles. In a multi-particle system, each particle has j has its own location r_j and mass m_j. The individual masses m_j then add up to the total mass.

$$M = \sum m_j$$

The center of gravity can also be calculated from the locations and masses of the individual particles. R can also be calculated. It is defined by

$$RM = \sum r_j m_j$$

Or directly as:

$$R = \frac{1}{M} \sum r_j m_j$$

The multi-particle system can therefore also be viewed in simplified terms. It has the mass M and is located at the place R.

One example is a molecule, which consists of several atoms. Each atom has its own mass m_j and its location r_j. The mass M of the molecule is the sum of the individual masses. The location R of the molecule is the center of gravity of the multi-particle system, in which all locations are mass-weighted.

Incidentally, the formula is very similar to the calculation of the expected value in stochastics. In the expected value, the result values of an experiment are weighted with the probabilities; here, location values are weighted with the masses. The center of gravity can therefore be interpreted as the mean value of the locations.

Velocity and momentum of multi-particle systems

The overall system also has a velocity: the change of its location $\dot{R} = \frac{dR}{dt}$ of its position with time. If the masses do not change, the following applies:

$$\dot{R} = \frac{1}{M} \sum \dot{r}_j m_j$$

The total velocity is therefore the (mass-weighted) average of the individual velocities.

What applies to the total momentum P? Here applies $P = \dot{R}M = \sum \dot{r}_j m_j = \sum p_j$. The total momentum P of the multi-particle system is therefore the sum of the individual momentums p_j. If the sum of the individual momentums is preserved, then the total momentum is also preserved.

As you can see: The center of gravity makes it possible to relate the properties of components to the properties of the overall system. The overall system now has a location, an overall speed, an overall mass and an overall momentum.

The center of gravity is based on the weighting of the individual components due to their inertia. The center of gravity has the property that the system as a whole behaves as if the entire mass were located there. The movement of the center of gravity follows the law of conservation of momentum.

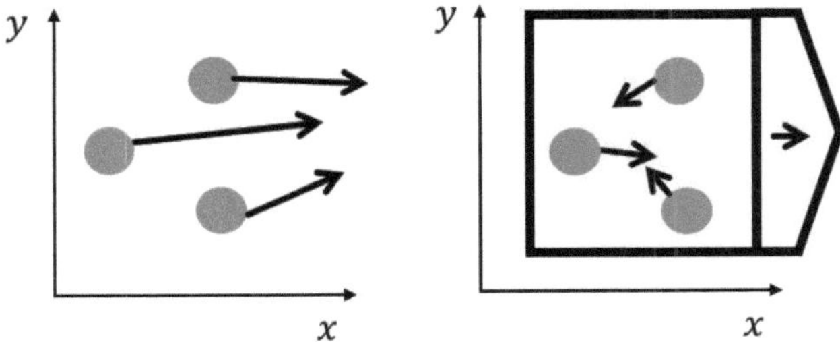

Figure 10: On the left you can see the movements of the individual particles. On the right are the movements relative to the center of gravity, as well as the movement of the center of gravity of the overall system.

With these new terms, we can now solve a major problem: Since there is no such thing as an excellent inertial frame, all location and velocity data must always be seen relative to an inertial frame. Therefore, momentum and energy also have no absolute values, but always depend on the inertial frame.

In a multi-particle system, however, there is a special place and a special speed. These are the center of gravity and the speed at which it moves. If you choose this as the inertial frame, then you can view the system from its own center, so to speak. You now obtain values that are characteristic of the system.

Unfortunately, this does not provide any new insights into momentum, as all momentums cancel each other out when viewed from the center of gravity. This is precisely the special feature of the center of gravity, that it represents a kind of mean value, and its movement also represents the mean value of the individual movements.

However, the concept of kinetic energy is much more productive.

The internal energy of multi-particle systems

We can look at the kinetic energy of all particles from the center of gravity.

Each particle j of the multi-particle system with the mass m_j has a velocity v_j. This can then be used to determine the kinetic energy of j. particle can then be determined.

$$E_{kin,j} = \frac{1}{2} m_j v_j^2$$

If you add up the energies of all the particles, you get:

$$E_{kin} = \sum E_{kin,j} = \sum \frac{1}{2} m_j v_j^2$$

What is special about this value? There is obviously a lot of kinetic energy in the system, even though it is at rest from the center of gravity and has zero velocity.

A multi-particle system has more kinetic energy than one would expect when looking at the overall movement. This invisible part is therefore called the **internal energy**.

This term is probably the central concept of thermodynamics and therefore also of chemistry.

In the case of momentum, we have already discussed that the speed of the center of gravity is something like a mass-weighted average of the individual movements. The formula for kinetic energy, on the other hand, is reminiscent of the dispersion of velocities. A high internal energy means that the individual velocities deviate strongly from the mean value, i.e. have a high velocity relative to the center of gravity.

So how does the inner energy come about?

Dissipative forces

In multi-particle systems, some of the energy can appear to disappear. This is exactly what happens with friction. However, the energy is not lost, but is distributed among the individual molecules and averages out when viewed macroscopically. The internal energy is therefore increased. This is why the energy is retained, but is no longer visible as kinetic or potential energy of the overall system.

The kinetic energy of objects can therefore be lost due to dissipative forces.

Energy that is visible in the system is distributed to the kinetic energy of the components in such a way that the effects cancel each other out and are no longer visible in the overall system.

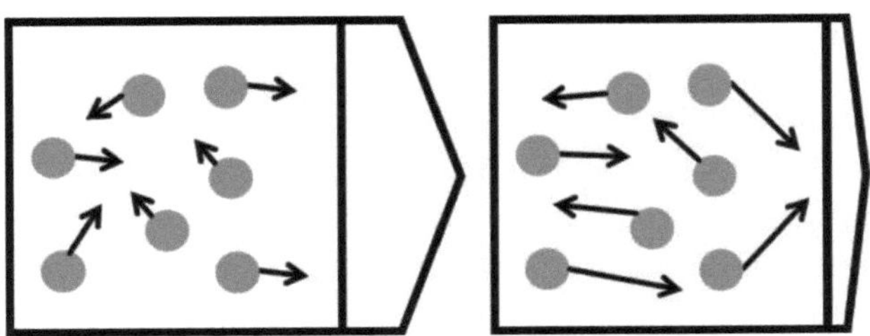

Figure 11: Dissipative forces lead to a reduction in the macroscopically visible directed kinetic energy. The energy is distributed to undirected individual movements.

Translations, Vibrations and Rotations

How can you imagine the internal energy? In the simplest case, you can see it in an explosion, like a supernova. The individual particles move away from the center at a very high speed, but the center of gravity of the entire system is still the same. This supernova as a whole does not move, and therefore has no kinetic energy when viewed from the center, although all particles move away from the center of gravity very quickly. These straight movements are called **translations**. But there are also other cases.

In addition to the kinetic energy of the particles, there is also the potential energy of the particles. The particles can attract each other. This force of attraction causes the velocities of the particles to decrease, eventually come to a standstill and the particles fly back again, just as a ball thrown upwards eventually returns. The same is known from a spring, where a moving mass is pulled back by the spring, passes the center and then moves in the other direction until the forces pull the mass back again.

This is exactly what **vibrations** are. Every particle can convert kinetic energy into potential energy and back again. This gives it a high energy, but it does not necessarily move away from the center of gravity as in an explosion.

In vibration, potential energy is converted into kinetic energy and back along a single dimension. The force acts along the axis in which the particle moves, i.e. like a spring. An example of vibration is the cyclic approach and repulsion of atoms in a molecule.

In **rotations**, on the other hand, the force acts perpendicular to the direction of movement, so that the particle changes direction and swings into a circular or elliptical orbit. This is typical for planetary orbits, around the sun, but also for rotational movements within molecules. The kinetic energy is not converted into potential energy, but is transferred from one spatial direction to another.

Both types of oscillations are caused by forces within a system. As the force and counterforce always cancel each other out, they have no effect on the center of gravity of a system or its movement.

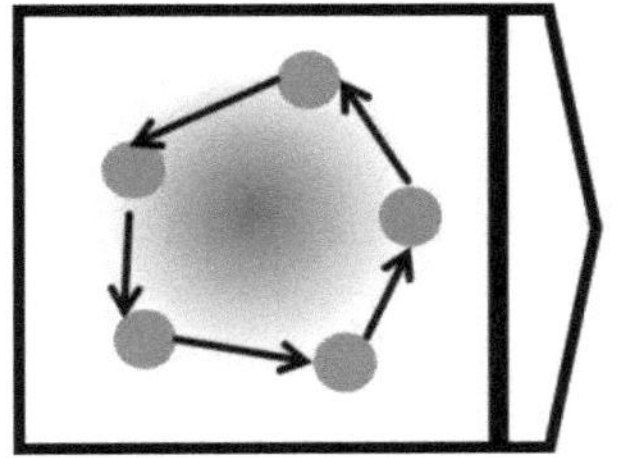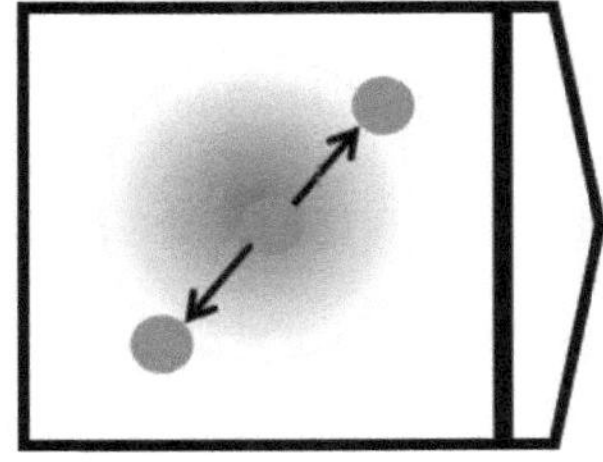

Figure 12: The potential energy of the system leads to the formation of rotations and vibrations. These contain internal energy that cannot be recognized macroscopically.

Degrees of freedom

The kinetic energy can therefore be present as translational, rotational or vibrational energy. Translations are straight movements of the particles in space, while the other two represent circular motions.

Let's imagine a container with gas molecules. Only the rectilinear movements of the translations ensure that the gas molecules collide with the wall and transfer energy in the form of work or heat. The rotations and vibrations within the gas atoms themselves also contain internal energy, but this does not contribute to an exchange.

So there is internal energy that has no influence on temperature or pressure and cannot be released by heat or work. (We will look at this in more detail in thermodynamics)

The number of degrees of freedom f describes the number of transition, vibration and rotation directions. If the kinetic energy is evenly distributed f degrees of freedom and there are only 3 spatial directions for translations, then the proportion that is $\frac{3}{f} E_{kin}$ is the proportion that can also be observed from the outside as translational energy.

Let's go back to the gas again. A freely moving n-atom molecule has 3n degrees of freedom, whereby only 3 degrees of freedom lie in the translational motion. The energy of translation is therefore only a small part of the internal energy in large molecules. The largest part is hidden in the internal vibrations and rotations.

5.2   The internal energy of the organization

The focus of the organization

In the following, we will understand an organization as an overall system that is recursively composed of business units, departments, teams and roles. Of course, each sub-organization has different values in the key figures. Nevertheless, it is possible to determine a value for the overall system.

Just as in physics, a center of gravity can be calculated by weighting and summing the individual contributions. Ultimately, this is a simple mean value calculation in which the contributions are weighted according to their inertia.

Inertia in sub-organization j	m_j
Key figure for sub-organization j	r_j
Total inertia = total mass M	$M = \sum m_j$
Center of Gravity R	$R = \dfrac{1}{M} \sum r_j m_j$
Total velocity $\dot{R}$	$\dot{R} = \dfrac{1}{M} \sum \dot{r}_j m_j$
Total momentum	$P = M \cdot \dot{R}$

The calculation is therefore simple and intuitively clear. You can calculate the equity per employee individually for two business units and obtain the weighted average as the center of gravity. The situation is similar for speed.

Now let's change the reference point and look at the entire system from the center of gravity. We are not interested in the absolute profit, but in how much the individual departments deviate from the average. There are better and worse performing departments. The results naturally average out because the center of gravity is our zero mark.

The inner energy of the organization

However, energy is where things get interesting. In terms of the center of gravity, we can see that some departments are improving or deteriorating compared to the average.

The internal energy expresses this in a number. It is calculated in the same way as the kinetic energy, but using the velocities relative to the center of gravity.

If our center of gravity represents the mean value, then the internal energy can be thought of as dispersion. A high internal energy therefore means that the individual departments deviate greatly from each other in their key performance indicators (such as profit/MA/year). If the internal energy were zero, then each department would have exactly the same results.

Where does this internal energy come from? Where do the deviations in the results come from?

The organization as a dissipative system

With the dissipative forces, we now have the reason why there are normally no straight, uniform movements. There is always something that slows down the normal process.

But what happens in organizations when there is friction? In the joint pursuit of a goal, each employee has to overcome different opposing forces. In the process, everyone's direction changes slightly and they deviate a little from the ideal direction. This results in differences and dispersion from the mean value. One employee is faster, the other slower. At the same time, movements occur that do not point in the direction of the target.

This friction slows down the movement of the organization and at the same time increases the internal energy.

The swinging organization

Where is this inner energy hidden? Are there also translations, vibrations and rotations in organizations? In all cases, the speeds average out. Nevertheless, they are different.

Translations correspond to the different speeds of the individual departments, which have a clear direction.

In the case of oscillations, i.e. vibrations and rotations, there is no clear direction of change. They are processes that ultimately always go round in circles. Results are sometimes better and sometimes worse. It is the internal fluctuations of the individual departments, i.e. their unevenness.

How does this come about? Internal reorganizations are one example. One time the focus is on the product, the next time on the region. If a department frequently changes its focus, then it changes its goals and goal achievement along with it. You can see that both customer proximity and product quality fluctuate. These cyclical fluctuations tie up energy because everyone is busy reorganizing. Despite all this, efforts go round in circles.

Of course, this is not to say that the reorganizations are generally pointless. We have already calculated out the forward movement in advance, and with the internal energy we have only investigated the part that is useless.

Degrees of freedom of the organization

There are therefore many degrees of freedom within an organization to which the internal energy can be distributed.

With translations, there is a clear, stable direction, at least for a partial organization. This direction does not exist for the degrees of freedom of the oscillations. It is a back and forth that has a high energy, but does not even lead to a change relative to the center of gravity of the organization.

What can be done practically with the oscillations and degrees of freedom of organizations? First of all, they cannot be measured empirically. But this is not possible in physics either. However, they do provide very good explanations about the nature of internal energy.

The heat capacity describes, for example, which temperature changes can be expected with which heat input. The temperature is only related to the energy in the translations and not to the energy of the vibrations. The more degrees of freedom a substance has, the less its temperature increases when heat is added. These terms can also be used to determine the degrees of freedom.

In the same way, the question arises as to which part of the energy supplied to an organization becomes visible again. The more degrees of freedom it has, the greater the proportion that is lost in internal vibrations.

5.3 Findings

What does this mean for organizations?

Organizations are complex, composite systems. They consist of business units, departments, teams and roles. This is why the classic law of conservation of energy falls short. There is such a thing as internal energy.

The internal energy says nothing about the current position or the change in the organization. The forward movement of the organization as a whole, i.e. the centre of gravity, has already been calculated in advance.

Internal energy is concerned with the dispersion of the departments' key figures in relation to the common average value.

There is a lot of energy in this dispersion, which does not contribute to the forward movement because the movements are undirected and average each other out.

In physics, we know that this part of the energy is much higher than the actual kinetic energy. It is precisely this energy that we want to understand and use.

Let's take a closer look at the internal energy of organizations. It consists of two components: The translations and the oscillations.

In the case of translations, sub-organizations have a clear course. They move in a certain direction with the key figures.

The speeds or directions of the oscillations change cyclically, so that everything goes round in circles.

The degrees of freedom now describe how many types of translations and oscillations there are. The proportion of translations is of particular interest because the energy contained therein can be used later.

6 Temperature

We now know the nature of the internal energy of the organization. It is created by looking at the organization from its centre of gravity and then taking an interest in the weighted scatter of speeds. How strongly do the results of the departments scatter from the average value?

By differentiating between the energies of translations, vibrations and rotations, we have already become more familiar with this phenomenon. Obviously, the translations in which changes go in a certain direction and do not run cyclically in a circle are of particular interest. We will now take a closer look at this part, but this time from a macroscopic perspective.

We therefore want to obtain a parameter of the overall organization that informs us about this proportion. This leads us to the temperature.

6.1 Temperature in physics

Temperature

A central intensive state variable of the thermodynamic system is the temperature. As an intensive variable, it expresses an average value.

The temperature is closely linked to the mean kinetic energy of the particles. The following applies:

$$< E_{kin} > = \frac{f}{2} k_B T$$

The expected value of the kinetic energy of a single particle (atom or molecule) depends on the temperature T, the number of degrees of freedom achievable at this energy f and the Boltzmann constant k_B.

The temperature can therefore be understood as a measure of the average kinetic energy of a single degree of freedom. It is therefore the proportion of the average energy that is present as translation and points in a specific spatial direction.

In a monatomic gas such as helium, for example, there are only three degrees of freedom of translation. There are three spatial directions, so $f = 3$. In a polyatomic molecule, on the other hand, the degrees of freedom can be significantly higher. Molecules can rotate or vibrate. At low energies, we still have solid bodies and this is not yet possible. These additional degrees of freedom only become accessible at higher energies. This becomes particularly clear during phase transitions from the solid to the liquid or gaseous state. During melting or boiling, new degrees of freedom are opened up. The system can therefore absorb energy without increasing the temperature. The energy is simply distributed to the new degrees of freedom.

Why is temperature such an important parameter? It indicates the proportion of energy that points in a certain direction as a translational movement. This proportion is later important for heat transfer on the wall of a vessel.

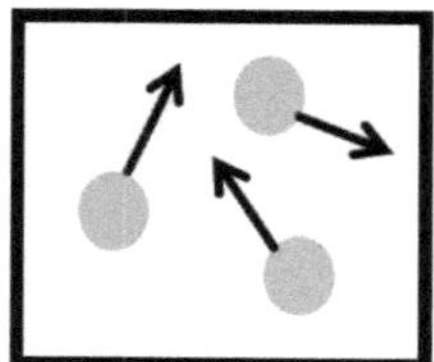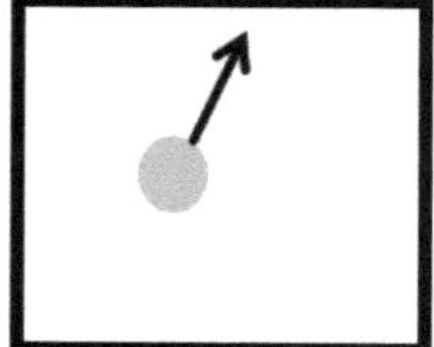

Figure 13: The temperature corresponds to the average kinetic energy of a particle per degree of freedom. It is not dependent on the particle density. Both systems have the same temperature.

An interesting aspect of temperature is the fact that it is based on the average kinetic energy of the particles, i.e. it is independent of the number of particles. For this reason, there can be high temperatures in the upper atmosphere even though there are only a few particles there.

Pressure

Pressure is defined as the force acting vertically on a surface, i.e.

$$p = F/A$$

What is the cause of the force acting on a surface? This is explained by the kinetic theory of gases. The cause of the force lies in the momentum of the particles. Particles can fly in different directions at different speeds. Some of the particles fly in the direction of the surface in question. Only those particles that are already close enough can reach the surface. When they hit the surface, they bounce back. This change in the sign of the velocity also leads to a change in the momentum of the particle, i.e. a force. Because of the law of interaction (actio = reactio), a force also acts on the wall, which accelerates it.

The explanation of the kinetic theory of gases also shows what can lead to high pressure. It takes many particles, each of which has a high momentum. The more particles there are, the more mass they have and the higher the speed, the higher the resulting force and therefore the pressure will be.

If the external pressure is greater than the internal pressure, a body is compressed. In the opposite case, it expands.

What happens if the pressure of the environment is different on several sides of the system? The system is pushed back on one side while it expands on the other. It moves.

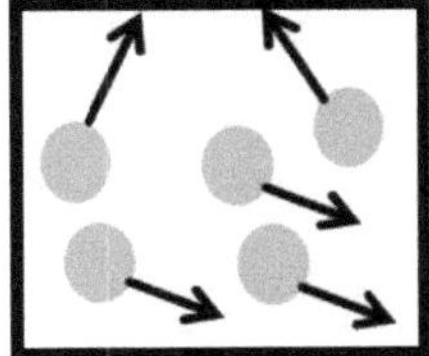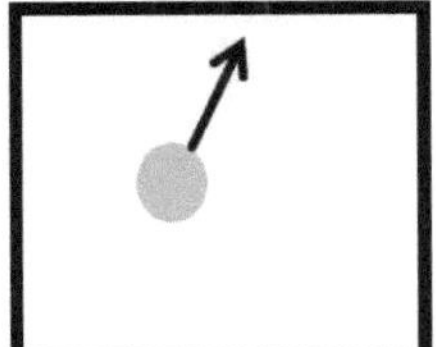

Figure 14: The pressure depends on both the kinetic energy and the particle density. The pressure is different here.

In contrast to temperature, pressure depends on momentum and particle density. In the upper atmosphere, the temperature is high but the air pressure is low.

Temperature and pressure are so-called **state variables**. They characterize the system. To be more precise, they are **intensive state variables** because they are contained in every point. If you connect two systems with the same temperature or pressure, these values are retained. The mean value has not changed. Examples of **extensive state variables,** on the other hand, would be the volume or the internal energy; when two systems are combined, the values add up.

Energy exchange

With pressure and temperature, we have now discussed two important intensive state variables. Both variables have a strong connection to the process variables work and heat.

Pressure difference and work

In the case of work, there is a pressure difference between the system and the environment. Since pressure is defined as force per area, this means that there is a force difference which leads to a change in volume. The **work** is then defined as the product of pressure and volume, or equivalently force times distance.

Temperature difference and heat

In the case of **heat**, there is a temperature difference between the system and its surroundings. This is equalized so that the system ultimately has the same temperature as its surroundings. The so-called thermal energy is transferred during equalization.

Energy balance

Work and heat are forms of energy transfer between a system and its environment. They represent certain types of energy transfer and both have the unit of energy. We can therefore draw up a balance. The internal energy is an extensive state variable that remains in the system if no changes are made by process variables such as heat and work.

These process variables are closely related to the intensive state variables of the system (temperature or pressure), which specify average values. If the intensive state variables of the system and the environment differ, they balance each other out. This results in a flow of energy into or out of the system, which changes the internal energy accordingly.

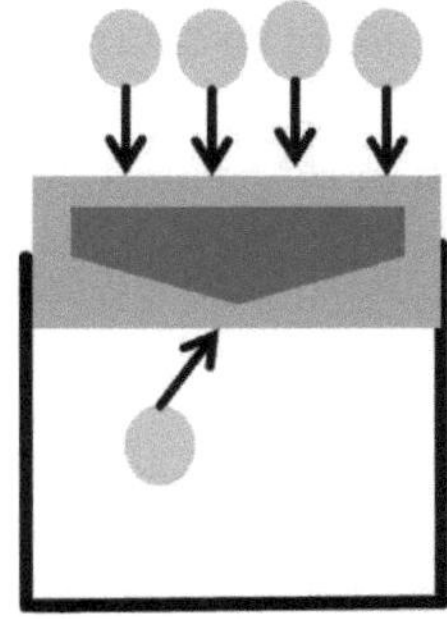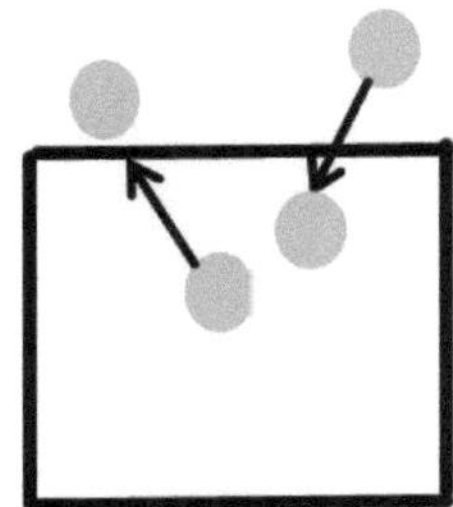

Figure 15: Work means that the volume is changed by a pressure difference. Heat is an energy transfer caused by a temperature difference.

6.2   The temperature of the organization

The operating temperature

Organizations have internal energy that can be distributed over many degrees of freedom. This corresponds to the numerous movements, rotations and vibrations that do not contribute to the overall movement of the organization.

How can you imagine the operating temperature? As in physics, it is the proportion of the average internal energy that points in a certain direction.

Since the organization is in the space of ratios, it means that the operating temperature is that part of the average internal energy that relates to a specific ratio.

The temperature indicates how strong the average scattering of a department is with regard to a velocity coordinate (e.g. profit/employee/year).

High operating temperatures show that there are large deviations from the average value. Half of them are better, the other half worse than the average value. In the end, of course, it averages out.

However, we have already seen that many degrees of freedom only represent oscillations. If there are many of these internal degrees of freedom, the temperature is lower and therefore the scatter in the respective key figure is also lower.

Pressure

Forces act on an organization from different sides of the environment. Where do these forces come from? They arise from interactions with stakeholders, i.e. with customers, suppliers, investors and employees. These interactions result in an exchange.

Customers expect products at a low price. Suppliers, on the other hand, want to achieve a high price for materials and tools. Employees want a high salary and investors want a high return.

If you take the current prices, salaries and returns as key figures for the organization, you can see that the organization cannot occupy arbitrary positions. There is a limit, which is influenced by the respective stakeholders.

If we look at the key figures as an interval, one side is obviously limited and the other is not. Employees are happy to accept a salary that is too high, and investors are also happy for unexpectedly high returns. The space in the coordinate is therefore a half-open interval. This is comparable to the Earth's atmosphere, where the gas envelope is limited only from the underside; the oceans also have a limited underside and negligible pressure from the upper side. However, there are practical limitations, as some combinations of high costs and yields are not feasible at low prices. As a result, there is a set of combinations of ratios that can be realized. This space has a volume. Each of the values in it would satisfy all stakeholders and is theoretically feasible.

Of course, the organization cannot fulfil all wishes and tries to push the boundaries. Stakeholders try to do the same. Pressure is exerted from both sides until the pressures are balanced.

Energy exchange

What is work now? The pressure from the markets is greater and the organization has to give way, which shifts these key figures to its disadvantage. Naturally, this situation is unpleasant and the organization is under increased stress in order to satisfy everyone. This increased stress is passed on from the sales department to the internal departments, similar to passing on the pressure. The technical departments have to make savings. There are now internal negotiations about who has to contribute how much. In the end, there is a balance here too.

This transfer of stress also increases the internal energy of the organization.

What about heat? Heat is an energy that comes from outside and causes the undirected internal energy to increase. The reason is the temperature difference. After all, temperature was a measure of the average dispersion of a department per key figure.

If one department has very different results in the quality of its intermediate products, this also has an effect on other departments. The variation is transferred and creates problems in the other departments. Conversely, well-organized departments try to educate their internal suppliers. Over a longer period of time, departments become similar. To a certain extent, this is a regression to the mean. The same phenomenon also occurs in teams, where the under- and overperformers are more oriented towards the average (albeit for different reasons).

An organization also has these relationships with stakeholders at the external boundary. Strong fluctuations have an effect and propagate. This effect corresponds to heat transfer, which ensures that different temperatures (i.e. scattering) equalize.

6.3 Findings

Thermodynamics leads to some new concepts.

The **temperature** is the average internal energy that relates to an average key figure. It describes the dispersion of the departments in a key figure.

The **pressure is** particularly evident in interactions with stakeholders such as customers, suppliers, employees and investors. It is easily recognizable in key figures such as unit price, salaries or returns, where the organization and stakeholders want to push the values in different directions.

Work is created by a **pressure difference**. If the above-mentioned ratios shift, the possible range for the ratios is reduced and the volume decreases. This external pressure is passed on to the inside, so that the internal pressure also increases and both sides are equalized.

Heat is generated by a **temperature difference**, i.e. by a different degree of variation among the participants. Departments with high fluctuations in quality also generate fluctuations in others. Conversely, departments with little variation in results try to influence others. In the end, different departments converge to a mean value.

7 Entropy

With the concepts from the last chapter, we are well prepared to face a central concept of thermodynamics: entropy.

Entropy is often understood as a measure of disorder. The second law states that disorder continues to increase. Anyone who works in organizations or has children can confirm this.

Now you could ask yourself: Why is disorder increasing? If disorder always increases, does it stop at some point, is there a maximum order or disorder? How orderly are we actually compared to these extreme values? And above all: how do you manage to get out of this maelstrom?

To answer these questions, we need to take a closer look at the nature of entropy in order to be able to translate it and some other very valuable terms.

7.1 Entropy in physics

Entropy is a colorful term. It is used in information theory, but also in thermodynamics. There are two different definitions in thermodynamics. We will go through all three variants. The first variant comes from information theory, and therefore from mathematics.

Micro and macro states

So let's start with the simplest example from combinatorics. We toss a coin. The result can be either heads (H) or tails (T). Both occur with a probability of 50%.

How many possible outcomes are there if you toss 10 coins at the same time? There are $|\Omega| = 2^{10} = 1024$.

Now let's take a look at how many possibilities there are for exactly k times head to occur in a throw. These are $\binom{10}{k}$ possibilities. The number of possibilities that 0 times head occurs, i.e. everything is a number, is $\binom{10}{0} = 1$. There is also only one possibility that everything is heads, i.e. $\binom{10}{10} = 1$.

However, there are $\binom{10}{5} = \frac{10\cdot9\cdot8\cdot7\cdot6}{1\cdot2\cdot3\cdot4\cdot5} = 252$ possibilities that there are just as many heads as tails.

In the terminology of statistical physics, the individual result corresponds to a **microstate**. In our example, there are therefore a total of 2^{10} microstates.

The event "X=k", that the result head occurs exactly k times, is a **macro state**. There is therefore the macro-state "X=5", to which 252 micro-states belong, and another macro-state "X=0", which has only one micro-state. The number of microstates belonging to a macrostate reflects its probability.

$$P(X = 5) = \frac{252}{1024}, \; P(X = 0) = \frac{1}{1024}, P(0 \le X \le 10) = \frac{1024}{1024} = 1.$$

Entropy H in information theory is about the question of how many microstates a macrostate has. As the number can be very large, the logarithm is always used. Computer scientists naturally use the logarithm to the base 2.

$$H(0 \le X \le 10) = ld\, 2^{10} = 10 \cdot ld2 = 10.$$

What is the entropy of the other macro-states?

$$H(X = 0) = ld \binom{10}{0} = ld\, 1 = 0$$

$$H(X = 5) = ld \binom{10}{5} = ld\, 252 \cong ld\, 256 = ld\, 2^8 = 8$$

The entropy of a system in a macro-state therefore logarithmically describes the number of associated micro-states. The higher the entropy, the more likely the macro-state is to be found. If the entropy increases by one, there are twice as many microstates. The corresponding macro-state is twice as likely as the previous one.

So this is about combinatorics and probability theory. If a macro-state can be realized by many more micro-states than all the others, then it has a much higher probability of being encountered. The entropy indicates logarithmically how many microstates belong to a macrostate.

Entropy in thermodynamics

The definition of entropy S in thermodynamics is slightly different to entropy H in information theory. This is mainly due to the fact that there are many more particles involved than in the example with the 10 coins.

The entropy S in thermodynamics is again a logarithmic measure of the number of possible microstates Ω that match the current macrostate.

$$S = k_B \cdot \ln |\Omega|$$

Since there are so many particles involved, this huge number is still too large even after forming the natural logarithm and is therefore multiplied by the Boltzmann constant $k_B = 1{,}38 \cdot 10^{-23} \frac{J}{K}$ which also gives the entropy S is given the unit Joule/Kelvin.

Let's take a closer look at the formula. There are $|\Omega|$ possibilities to distribute the energy to the different particles and their degrees of freedom, so that the observed internal energy, temperature and pressure are obtained macroscopically.

Here too, entropy is a measure of ambiguity or ambiguity. It indicates how much information is missing in order to be able to deduce the correct microstate from known macro variables. The higher the number of microstates, the higher the probability and the higher the entropy.

At high entropy there are many possible microstates, at low entropy there are only a few, and at zero entropy there is only one. As a result, macro-state A with high entropy is much more likely than macro-state B with low entropy. In large systems, the effect is so strong that only a single macro-state can be observed in the steady state.

Entropy - Macroscopic

We have now become familiar with the statistical definition of entropy. In classical thermodynamics, the same term is introduced differently.

The entropy change is defined as the ratio of the reversibly added heat and the absolute temperature.

$$dS = \frac{Q_{rev}}{T}$$

Only small changes that can be reversed immediately are reversible.

This entropy change is noticeable during melting or boiling, for example. During these phase transformations, heat is added from outside, but the absolute temperature does not change.

Melting 1 mol of ice to water at 0°C = 273 K with a thermal energy of 273 J produces exactly the entropy change

$$dS = 1\,JK^{-1}mol^{-1}$$

When heat is added, the internal energy and therefore the mean kinetic energy increases. Why does the temperature not increase during melting? It is because new degrees of freedom are created at this temperature. Water molecules are no longer trapped in the lattice of the ice crystal, but can move more freely. During melting, the energy is distributed to these new degrees of freedom. This results in rotations and vibrations that do not contribute to the temperature. When the ice has melted, the temperature rises again (with increased heat capacity)

This classic definition of entropy therefore states that the energy supplied is distributed over different degrees of freedom. If the temperature remains constant as the mean kinetic energy per degree of freedom, then new degrees of freedom must obviously have been added.

Now that we have examined entropy from all angles, we can move on to the central statements of thermodynamics.

The four laws of thermodynamics

Analogous to Newton's laws, there are the four main laws of classical thermodynamics.

The **Zeroth Law** states: If two bodies A and B have the same temperature, and B and C have the same temperature, then A and C also have the same temperature. The temperature is therefore an equivalence relation.

$$T(A) = T(B), \qquad T(B) = T(C) \quad \Rightarrow \quad T(A) = T(C)$$

The **first law** stems from the conservation of energy. The internal energy of an isolated system is conserved.

$$\frac{dU}{dt} = 0$$

The first law therefore states that internal energy only changes if there is an exchange of energy between the system and its environment. It follows directly from the law of conservation of energy. One example is the transfer of energy through work or heat.

The **second law** states that the entropy of an isolated system cannot decrease.

$$\frac{dS}{dt} \geq 0$$

The **third law** states that the entropy at absolute zero is also zero.

$$T = 0 \implies S = 0$$

Let's take a closer look at the second law. It states that the entropy of an isolated system constantly increases until a maximum is reached.

So why does entropy increase? In a thermodynamic system, molecules constantly collide and transfer energy in the process. Some molecules speed up, some slow down. You now have a different microstate, which may belong to a different macrostate.

Similar to tossing coins, the system assumes the more probable macro-states. The larger the system is, the more dominant a single macro-state is. It is precisely this state that is adopted after a long period of time. This state is then called the equilibrium state, as it no longer changes. It has the maximum entropy, i.e. the highest probability.

Let's imagine a piece of metal. It is possible that the left side glows and the right side has absolute zero temperature. However, particles constantly collide with each other and then transfer momentum and energy. It would be theoretically possible for the temperature on the left and right to be different despite all this. But it is extremely unlikely. On the other hand, there are many more ways of distributing the energy equally on both sides. This most probable state is also assumed at some point. This is also the deeper reason why the temperatures equalize and the energy flows from one side to the other.

The increase in entropy is not only the cause of the flow of energy, but also of the flow of matter. If you bring two liquids together, they mix because there are more microstates where they are mixed than where they are separated.

Aiming for a higher entropy is therefore both the trigger for energy to be transferred from one place to another and for concentrations to equalize. This always continues until the macro-state with the highest entropy is reached: the **state of equilibrium.**

The Boltzmann distribution

Let's take a closer look at the equilibrium state. It is the most probable macro-state of a system, and therefore the most interesting. How is the internal energy distributed here?

Let's take N particles with the total energy E. Each particle contains a part of this energy. Let's say there are only k different energy levels e_1 up to e_k that a particle can have. Here $N = \sum n_j$ is the total number of particles and $E = \sum e_j n_j$ is the total energy.

How many ways are there to distribute the total energy E among the N particles?

The Boltzmann distribution now states that the following relationship applies in a very large system in a state of equilibrium:

$$\frac{n_i}{N} = \frac{1}{q} \cdot \exp\left(-\frac{e_i}{k_B T}\right), \qquad wobei \ q = \sum_j \exp\left(-\frac{e_j}{k_B T}\right)$$

Where k_B is again the Boltzmann constant and T the absolute temperature.

Let's go through this formula step by step. The proportion of particles $\frac{n_i}{N}$ that have the energy level e_i is proportional to the expression in the exponential function. One can $\frac{n_i}{N}$ can also be interpreted as the probability that, if a particle is selected at random, one with the energy e_i is obtained. You can see from the exponential function that this probability is lower the greater the e_i is. This is why there are only a few particles with high energies, but many with low energy.

The exact distribution depends on only one variable: the temperature T. If the temperature T is increased, then the proportion of high energy contributions and consequently also the average value is increased.

The pre-factor q is the normalization, so that the sum of the probabilities is exactly 1.

Within the equilibrium state, this is the most probable distribution. However, we know nothing about the microstates because they change with every collision.

The Boltzmann distribution is based purely on combinatorics. There are few objects with high energy, but many with low energy. The distribution depends on a single parameter: the temperature.

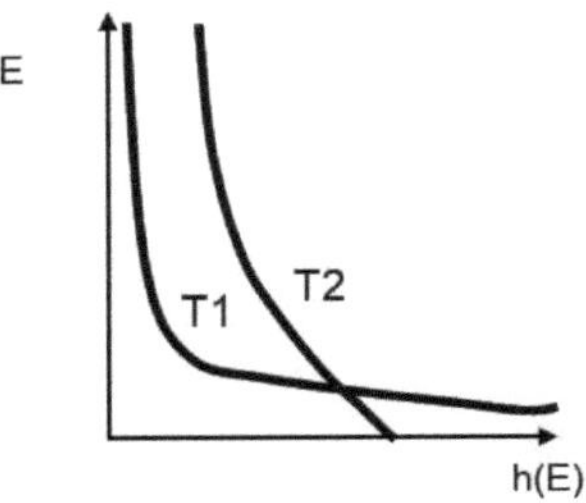

Figure 16: The Boltzmann distribution shows the frequency of occupancy of energy levels depending on the temperature. At the high temperature T2, the high energy levels are occupied more frequently than at the low temperature T1.

Free energy

We now know that the entropy of a system continues to increase until a state of equilibrium is reached. During this development, the system changes, but not afterwards. This ability to change can also be quantified. It is the Gibbs energy of a system. It indicates how far away the system is from a state of equilibrium.

A system with the internal energy U has a certain number of particles N, a volume V and an entropy S. The pressure p and the temperature T are constant.

We have already seen that with the constant external pressure p the work $W = -p \cdot dV$ is released to achieve an increase in volume. dV is achieved. We can now ask ourselves how much work was necessary to go from zero volume to the current volume? It is $W = -pV$. The internal energy decreases during expansion, so the value is negative. If no energy comes from outside, then part of the internal energy is responsible for maintaining the current volume despite the external pressure.

If we are not interested in this part of the internal energy, which only serves to maintain the volume, we can use enthalpy. The term is particularly useful in chemistry, where the energy required to expand liquids is sometimes ignored. This aspect is simply factored out. The **enthalpy** is:

$$H = U - W = U + pV$$

The situation is similar for temperature and entropy. How much heat Q is necessary to build up the high number of microstates with entropy T to build up the high number of microstates with entropy S? It is $Q = ST$.

Obviously, part of the internal energy U is necessary to build up the current volume and entropy. This part of the internal energy is only responsible for maintaining the volume and entropy and cannot be used for other tasks.

If you subtract these summands from the internal energy, you get the **free enthalpy** G, which is also called **Gibbs energy.**

$$G = U + pV - TS$$

The Gibbs energy is therefore the part of the energy that cannot yet be explained by the macro state. However, as the entropy S increases continuously, the Gibbs energy G decreases accordingly until it is zero. Then the maximum entropy is reached and the system is in a state of equilibrium.

A note on naming: Gibbs energy is often referred to as **free energy** in biology. We use the term free energy from here on.

Free energy is therefore the proportion of internal energy that is (freely) available for change. If the free energy is zero, there are no more macroscopically observable changes and the state of equilibrium is reached. In an isolated system, the free energy decreases permanently because the entropy increases. This continues until the free energy is zero and the maximum entropy is reached. In order to obtain further free energy, it must therefore be imported from outside.

7.2   The entropy of the organization

Entropy in the organization

So what is entropy in organizations? Let's remember: entropy is a measure of how many ways a system can be realized, of which certain macroscopic properties are known.

What would be a macro state? A macro state would be, for example, that the organization achieves a certain profit X. Every way in which the organization can work would then be a micro state.

Of course, both levels are connected. Many ways of working, i.e. many micro-states, lead to the same macro-state and thus to the same overall success.

However, there are a much higher number of opportunities to remain unsuccessful and not make a profit than opportunities that lead to an outstanding profit. The higher the desired profit, the fewer opportunities there are to achieve it.

The probability of making no or little profit is therefore higher than making a high profit. There are simply too many ways to go wrong.

A simple practical example is file storage. There are only a few ways to correctly name, version and store files in the right place, but many more ways to do it wrong. When a new employee files a file, the micro-states, i.e. the types of naming and the filing locations, are all equally likely. But the macro state "correctly named and filed" has fewer microstates than the macro state "file is incorrectly named or filed".

Such phenomena accumulate in an organization, so that even the macro state of "high profit" is less likely than "low profit".

The entropy of a macro-state of the organization is now a logarithmic measure of the number of these possibilities.

Entropy and variety

In complexity theory, the term variety is also used instead of entropy. Variety also indicates the number of possibilities logarithmically. Ashby has shown that it is necessary to have a certain internal variety in order to be able to react to the variety of the outside world. Only variety can absorb variety. In this sense, high entropy is not always bad. In Stafford Beer's Viable System Model, the question is precisely how this variety can be controlled. When does a sub-organization need many degrees of freedom, when should everything be very strict and optimized? However, this exciting question is probably a topic for another book.

Entropy of the organization viewed from a different angle

Let us remember the other definition of entropy. A change in entropy also corresponds to the ratio of the energy supplied to the temperature. We saw that during melting, the temperature remains the same and the number of degrees of freedom increases.

In an organization, you sometimes notice that adding energy has no effect. Why is that? Perhaps new degrees of freedom are being developed and the energy is being distributed among them.

This is the case, for example, when new employees join a team. But the output still doesn't increase. Where has the energy gone? In the newly created degrees of freedom of rotation and vibration. Larger teams first have to find each other and deal with themselves.

Let's think back to the example of heat capacity. We worked for 40 hours and spent an average of 4 hours working towards a goal. The heat capacity had a value of 10. Now we are reorganizing. Everyone has been given different responsibilities. We don't know our new colleagues yet. The next week we work 60 hours, but still only 4 hours per target. Why is that? There were new tasks. We first had to get to know everyone. That increased the number of internal degrees of freedom. These tie up energy that is not visible to the outside world.

The second law for organizations

The second law of thermodynamics for organizations states that entropy continues to increase until a state of equilibrium is reached.

However, this sentence only applies if the organization is isolated, i.e. has no energy exchange with the environment. This is practically never the case because organizations constantly interact with people and other organizations such as customers, suppliers and investors. But we have already seen several times that it is important to start with idealized conditions in order to mirror and better evaluate the real phenomena.

Why does entropy increase? It is simply because the macro-states with higher entropy are more likely.

Let's go back to our file storage. It's finally tidy. Everything is perfectly filed. Almost uniquely perfect. Entropy is therefore zero because there is only one state of perfection and the logarithm of one is zero. Now the dear colleagues come and start filing new files again. Entropy increases again.

Of course, the files are not stored randomly in reality. But it takes energy to formulate these rules, to communicate them and to ensure that they are observed. If you invest this energy, entropy increases more slowly. Tidying up itself also cost energy and apparently even reduced entropy. It always costs energy to counteract the increasing entropy.

Distribution

Let's consider a large, balanced organization in a state of equilibrium that has a certain amount of internal energy. How is this energy distributed among the employees? How can this be expressed?

Since the Boltzmann distribution is a purely mathematical statement that does not originate from observations in nature, we can easily transfer it.

It examines a system with an internal energy E and N components, and asks how the energy is distributed among these components in a state of equilibrium. Energy is constantly transferred between the components. There is also a minimum energy that cannot be undercut.

For us, the system is the organization and the components are the departments, teams or roles. The Boltzmann distribution states that only a few components have a very high energy and many have a low or minimal energy.

Let's remember the definition of internal energy again. We have interpreted it as the dispersion of velocities relative to the average. Thus Boltzmann means that most departments have a low energy and are therefore close to the average. There are a few that deviate strongly from the average. However, this applies to both sides, i.e. both the underperformers and the overperformers.

The Boltzmann distribution also shows that the exact ratio of these groups depends on a single parameter, the temperature. In the case of the organization, we will call this the operating temperature.

The higher the operating temperature, the greater the dispersion, of course, and the greater the proportion of departments that are far from the average. Both sides are interesting. The underperformers have the opportunity to improve. With the overperformers, you can overcome existing limits and create something new.

However, no matter how high this operating temperature is. Even in a state of equilibrium, there is always a distribution, and some parts carry more internal energy than others.

Free energy

We have become familiar with the concept of free energy. It is the part of the inner energy that is not yet in balance and therefore usable.

The free energy is calculated by subtracting two terms from the internal energy.

Firstly, organizations have to withstand pressure from the outside world, in particular the expectations of stakeholders. Investors always want higher returns, customers want lower prices, suppliers want higher prices and employees want higher salaries. These key figures are therefore subject to one-sided limitations imposed by stakeholders. Market prices are set in the various markets. Here, the forces of the partners are in balance. The organization needs energy to expand the range of its permitted KPI values.

Secondly, organizations have a certain complexity. It must be maneuverable and therefore needs a variety of options in order to reach its goal. It therefore needs a certain entropy.

The portion of an organization's total energy that is necessary to withstand market pressure and maintain internal diversity must therefore be deducted. Because this part only maintains the status quo in the current environment. It merely allows business as usual.

The remaining energy is then the free energy with which the organization can create something new and change.

You are probably familiar with this. A large part of the energy is used to meet the requirements of the stakeholders and to be halfway able to work. Only a small part is really free.

7.3 Findings

Organizations are complex, and as an outsider you can only observe a few aspects. These distinguishable states are the **macro-states**. Each of these has a different number of realizations, the **micro-states**.

Entropy is a logarithmic measure of the number of microstates and therefore ambiguity that belong to a macrostate. In organizations, it describes the number of possible courses of action that ultimately lead to the same result. High entropy means that there are practically many alternative courses of action. With low energy, there are very few options. The entropy for the "high profit" macro-state is therefore much lower than for the "low profit" macro-state.

The **second law of thermodynamics** states that entropy cannot decrease in an isolated system. In other words: at some point, a system assumes its most probable macro-state. Then it is in equilibrium.

The **equilibrium state is** the macro state that is observed in most cases when business as usual prevails.

The **distribution** now shows how the internal energy of an organization in a state of equilibrium is distributed across its departments, teams and roles. Many of them have low internal energy and are therefore close to the average. On the other hand, a few have very high energy and are therefore far from the average. However, this applies to underperformers as well as overperformers, as it does not matter in which direction you deviate in terms of energy. The exact distribution depends on just one parameter: the temperature. If the temperature is higher, the proportion of those who deviate strongly from the average increases.

The **free energy** indicates how much energy an organization still has left to create something new. This part of the energy is not necessary to maintain the current expansion on the market or the current intrinsic complexity. The bad news is that every organization strives for a state of equilibrium in which precisely this free energy is zero. This is exactly the thermodynamic equilibrium, also known as heat death. In other words, an organization expands into new markets and creates so much internal complexity along the way that it becomes incapable of acting. Why does it do this? Because it can. It is simply a result of pressure and temperature equalization. The consequence of this is that the organization must constantly import new energy in order to regain its ability to act.

One more remark:

The second law suggests that entropy continues to increase and therefore the unlikely case of success does not occur. However, this is only half the truth: growing entropy is not the opponent of order, but quite the opposite: it is also the only driving force that creates order. Because it is the only driving force at all. To achieve this, the force of increasing entropy only needs to be elegantly diverted to create a negative energy change. This is precisely the fine art of all living beings. But more on that later.

8   Structures and transformations

Mechanics and thermodynamics explain the rules by which the world works. But it is only when we focus on atoms and molecules that things become really concrete. This is where these rules of the game manifest themselves.

Stable structures are created by particles being held together by attractive forces. The stronger these attractive forces are, the more stable the structures are.

In chemistry, it is important to understand the strength of these bonds. In a chemical reaction, an existing stable structure must always be destroyed before the individual parts can assemble to form another stable structure.

This approach is of course highly relevant for organizations. What are stable structures? How stable are they? How do you manage to create a new stable structure in the event of a change that does not immediately fall apart again?

So let's start by taking a closer look at these stable structures.

8.1   The structures and transformations in chemistry

Structures

Matter is made up of atoms. The atoms themselves consist of an atomic nucleus and electrons. Before we can ask ourselves how chemical reactions take place and how fast they are, we should ask ourselves what keeps atoms or molecules stable in the first place.

There are four known interactions in nature: The strong and weak interaction, electromagnetism and gravity. These four interactions have different strengths and different ranges.

The protons and neutrons in the nucleus are held together by the strong interaction. At short distances, this is many times stronger than electromagnetism. This is why the protons stay together despite their repulsive positive charge. However, once the atomic nucleus reaches a certain charge, the nucleus disintegrates because the protons are too far apart and the electromagnetic repulsion is stronger than the attractive forces of the strong interaction.

However, this attraction between the protons means that the nucleus is positively charged. To compensate for this, the electron shell is formed so that the atom as a whole is uncharged.

Gravity, on the other hand, is significantly weaker than the other forces. Gravity causes atoms to attract each other, but they do not crash into each other because the electromagnetic repulsion of the two electron shells prevails from a certain distance. An equilibrium point is reached here. As a result, atoms in a solid have a certain distance between them.

There are attractive and repulsive forces with different strengths. In nested systems, the smallest components are the most stable because they are held together by the strongest forces. Higher system levels are less stable.

If a repulsive and an attractive force exactly balance each other out, there is no more acceleration and a fixed distance is maintained. Stable structures are the result of balancing forces.

Bonds

Chemistry mainly investigates structures such as atoms and molecules, which are held together by the electromagnetic force. The strong and weak interaction in the atomic nucleus usually plays just as little a role as the much weaker gravitational force.

Although electromagnetism is the only interaction here, it can still create bonds of varying strength.

The strongest bond is the bond between the electrons and the atomic nucleus, which balances out the positive nuclear charge.

Atoms can also combine to form molecules. These covalent bonds are strong, but can be chemically modified.

The bonds between the molecules are then somewhat weaker. They are created by the partial charges. One example is the hydrogen bond, in which the oxygen of a water molecule attracts the hydrogen atoms of another water molecule due to its high electronegativity. This type of attraction between molecules is already much weaker. When ice melts or water boils, these bonds are broken.

Even if there is only a single force, it can have a finely graduated effect. The gradation results from the fact that the forces on the lower levels do not balance each other out exactly, resulting in a slight imbalance.

Reactions

The atoms in molecules are held together by covalent bonds. The covalent bonds have a certain energy. This energy is independent of the chemical way in which the molecule was formed. If you start with the individual chemical elements, you can add up the energies of the transformations up to the finished molecule. This energy is the **standard enthalpy of formation of the molecule.** It is a state variable and expresses how much energy is contained in the bonds.

These covalent bonds are now changed during the chemical reaction. This does not take place in a single step, but follows a **reaction mechanism**. As the reactants are usually in a stable form, it initially costs energy to break this stability. Molecules give up or take up electrons. This results in an unstable intermediate state. In the second step, the products are then formed from this intermediate state.

The energy required for the first step comes from the kinetic energy of the particles that collide. This also shows the connection with the **Boltzmann distribution**. The higher the temperature, the more particles with high energy there are, and the higher the probability that this energy is sufficient to initiate a chemical reaction. This is why chemical reactions take place faster at high temperatures.

Dipole-dipole interactions

In addition to the strong covalent bonds, there is also the dipole-dipole interaction.

Even if a molecule has an overall neutral electrical charge, the individual charges it contains can be unevenly distributed. One side of the molecule is slightly more negative, the other slightly more positive. The result is a so-called dipole.

One example is the water molecule. In the molecule, an oxygen atom is covalently bonded to two hydrogen atoms. The molecule is electrically neutral. Due to the higher electronegativity of the oxygen, the water molecule has a negative partial charge on the oxygen side, while the hydrogen atoms have a positive partial charge.

These partial charges cause neighboring molecules to attract each other. In the case of water, this is called a hydrogen bond. Such a bond is significantly weaker than a covalent bond within the molecules. It therefore takes significantly less energy to break these bonds.

Long polymers such as proteins can fold through their own partial charges and thus take on a defined shape. The partial charges on the outside have characteristic profiles to which another molecule can dock. As the two molecules are held together by a large number of adjacent bonds, the bond strengths add up, resulting in a slightly stronger bond overall. As a result, proteins are temporarily connected to other molecules.

Dynamic equilibrium

In principle, processes such as chemical reactions can always take place in both directions. Reactants combine to form a product. At the same time, there is a decomposition of a product into its components at another point.

Each of the two directions occurs at a certain speed, which depends on the concentrations. The more products there are, the more can decompose.

If one of the two speeds is higher than the other, this results in a net turnover. This continues until the velocities are equal. This point is the dynamic equilibrium. The same amount is converted in one direction as in the reverse direction. The concentrations no longer change in total.

This **equilibrium** can be more on the reactant or product side. It then describes the ratio of reactants and products, which is established after a longer period of time and then remains stable. The equilibrium state has the highest entropy and is the macro-state with the highest probability.

If a mixing ratio is not yet in equilibrium, then the change in the direction of equilibrium is called **exergonic** or spontaneous. Changes in the opposite direction are called **endergonic**, i.e. not spontaneous.

Exergonic processes take place spontaneously because this increases entropy. The second law of thermodynamics states that the increase in entropy is the driving force of the universe. It causes endergonic reactions to take place. Endergonic reactions, on the other hand, require a decrease in entropy, which is not readily possible.

8.2 The structures and transformations in the organization

Structures of the organization

Organizations are made up of teams and roles that are filled by people. Now, not everything in an organization can be changed at will. Some changes cost more energy than others because the existing structures are maintained by strong forces.

There are very strong forces in personality traits such as introversion or extroversion. It would take a lot of energy to turn an introvert into an entertainer. The same also applies to other personality traits.

People's habits have somewhat weaker powers. Habits that have been practiced for a long time can be changed with a lot of patience. New habits emerge that are stable again. (The inner bastard corresponds to the energy difference between a stable state and an unstable transitional state of change)

The bonds between people in a team are no longer quite as strong. The ties between sub-organizations at a high level or to subsidiaries of the same group are becoming increasingly weaker. Therefore, reorganizations are often easier to implement than changing the behavior of many people.

If you want to change something in an organization, you have to remove these forces that maintain stability by using enough free energy.

Connections

So what are the atoms and molecules of the organization? If we think backwards from the biology translation of the catalyst, the best working conditions must be such a structure. This again consists of the production factors man, machine, material and method.

Humans exist physically as matter, they can contribute energy and they are carriers of information. In addition, they are naturally alive.

Tools can have different characteristics. A hammer has neither energy nor information. A PCB placement machine, on the other hand, contributes energy and information.

The material factor can also include matter, energy and information. Material is simply that which is changed in a process. Only the method is pure information, which is of course stored on a physical data carrier with or without energy.

Now you can build a catalyst from the factors of man, machine and method, which, when the material is added, accelerates a process. So what are the energy levels?

The practically unchangeable characteristics of people or tools are similar to atoms. They are not normally changed.

However, they can be permanently connected to each other. A person can permanently possess a certain know-how, a fixed workplace and a computer with installed software. This overall network is more like the level of a molecule. The structures can be built up and changed, but they should then remain stable in the long term.

The connection between people is somewhat more unstable. The flow of material in the process is also constantly changing. These are already weaker bonds.

Let's take a closer look at the different bond strengths.

Changing structures

What are structures in an organization that can be changed by the organization but are still stable? Let's start with the workplaces. We are talking about people who use tools to process material.

Let's take the example of an employee in an insurance company who processes applications. The employee's personality is not changed by the organization. However, the employee is at a personal workstation. She has a computer with a login and installed software. The employee also has a lot of experience with the processes and the software.

All of this is a stable combination of people, tools and methods. It takes free energy to build this network. Software is installed. The employee is trained.

If the software has good usability and the employee is used to it, the thought structures and user interfaces are a good match.

This is a strong bond that remains stable over a long period of time. If the software is changed, it takes a **lot of energy** to break away from the old and then rebuild the new. In particular, the things that worked well before and no longer work after the change are painful. After some time, however, a new stable environment is created again.

In order to bring about this change, you need **free energy**. If all energy is already being used to maintain the status quo, such a change is difficult to achieve.

The bonds must therefore be so stable that they cannot be destroyed unintentionally. However, a certain amount of free energy should be required. This in turn should not be too high, so that a change is not made impossible.

Weak ties

Let's stick with the example of the employee in the insurance company. She has a stable connection to her workplace and the software tools.

Let's imagine a customer comes into the office and wants to take out an insurance policy. To do this, the employee has to create the customer's master data and enter the contract details.

This data may initially be available in a different form. It takes free energy to put the data into the correct sequence. In the end, the employee has the data in her short-term memory and it is in the fields of the input screen.

So now the temporary connection to the customer has been established. Perhaps the employee needs to ask her colleague again, which results in another temporary connection. Of course, the employee remains stable with her workstation and the software, even if a customer has left. She may forget the data again.

The reciprocity with which colleagues help each other out is also a weak bond. However, the sum total of weak ties is what holds an organization together.

Dynamic equilibrium

In organizations, too, processes often take place in both directions. If an employee absorbs new information through a learning process, they can also forget the knowledge again.

If you look at many employees at the same time, there is a speed of learning and a speed of forgetting. The point at which both speeds are equal is the point of equilibrium, which occurs in the long term. The equilibrium point here shows how many people have a certain amount of knowledge.

The balance point is initially strongly on the side of not knowing. Unlearning happens spontaneously, i.e. exergonically. Learning, on the other hand, is not a spontaneous process and is therefore endergonic.

Unfortunately, this is the normal case. Building successful structures is usually endergon at first. If this were not the case, then the best working conditions would arise spontaneously without having to do anything. We will see later how such endergonic processes can nevertheless be accelerated.

8.3 Findings

Organizations are about creating and changing stable structures. The structures are maintained by ties, which can vary in strength.

It's like chemistry. Some structures, such as the atomic nucleus, are held together by such strong forces that they are practically unchangeable. Other interactions, such as gravity, are too weak to be ignored in most cases.

In the same way, you can look at the structures in bonds in organizations. Individual personality traits of people or properties of tools cannot practically be changed. Other bonds are too weak. So we are talking about medium-strength bonds that create stable structures, but which can also be changed again.

Strong ties are needed to keep people, tools and knowledge together in the long term. Employees have their workstation, computer with login and software. This structure should be established and permanently stable. Somewhat weaker bonds are created when several people work in a team. These bonds should be easier to change in order to react flexibly to new challenges.

The importance of non-functional requirements can be clearly seen in the various bindings. The usability of a software refers to establishing connections between the human and tool factors as easily as possible. Learnability is about a person being able to acquire knowledge quickly and memorize it permanently. The interoperability of systems simplifies the links between tools. All of this serves to create stable structures. Of course, flexibility is also expected from employees and tools. This refers to the ability to dissolve existing structures and build new ones. Ultimately, it is about how stable a structure is. It is a compromise between stability and changeability.

9 Negative entropy

So far, it has only been about which structures are stable at all, and that free energy is needed to change them. We have also seen that there is a dynamic balance between construction and decay, whereby the actual force of the universe, the increase in entropy, leads everything in the direction of decay.

Now let's focus on the speed of the processes. How fast do processes run? Can you influence the speed? How can non-spontaneous processes also be allowed to run?

This question is highly relevant in organizations. If an organization has to change, then this should happen quickly. On the other hand, an organization must also have processes that do not run on their own, i.e. spontaneously.

Chemical kinetics can answer all these questions.

9.1 The emergence of order in living beings

Kinetics

How quickly does a chemical reaction take place? That depends on how high the concentrations of the products and reactants are and how high the temperature is.

The **high concentration** means that the particles are closer together and therefore meet more frequently. This increases the speed.

The **high temperature** also means that particles move faster and therefore collide more frequently. In addition, they have a higher relative speed when they collide, i.e. a higher kinetic energy. We have already seen this distribution in the **Boltzmann distribution**. Due to the higher speed, the particles have enough kinetic energy when they collide to break up the existing stable structures and cause a chemical reaction.

The speed of processes depends on the temperature and concentration.

Unfortunately, concentrations tend to decrease because the increase in entropy ensures that all concentration differences are equalized.

Increasing the temperature increases the speed. However, it accelerates all chemical reactions equally. This makes the temperature unsuitable for triggering only certain reactions. Another mechanism, on the other hand, is much more selective.

Catalysis

How can you accelerate a chemical reaction very selectively? You need a catalyst. This increases the probability that two particles that fly towards each other with sufficient energy will meet at the right angle and enter into a reaction.

During the reaction, the catalyst combines briefly with the reactants before they combine with each other. This enables a different reaction process that requires less free energy. Due to the Boltzmann distribution, there are then many more reactants that have the necessary energy.

The special thing about catalysts is that they are very specific and only work in certain reactions and not in others. The energy required can therefore be used in a very targeted manner.

Cells build enzymes as catalysts for each of their chemical reactions. Many of the enzymes can also be switched on and off individually. In this way, a cell can determine exactly which reactions should take place and which should not.

However, a catalyst does not change the equilibrium point. It accelerates both the forward and reverse direction of a reaction. This therefore only leads to the equilibrium point being reached more quickly. This means that only spontaneous, i.e. exergonic, processes take place in which free energy is reduced. Endergonic processes do not take place.

Energetic coupling

A catalyst can therefore accelerate very specific exergonic processes. However, there are many reactions in a cell that are endergonic. For example, DNA must be produced from nucleotides. This process does not occur spontaneously. How is this possible?

There are two possibilities here. In the case of DNA, an exergonic process is directly linked to an endergonic process. DNA synthesis is endergonic, i.e. it does not occur spontaneously. At the same time, however, ATP breaks down exergonically to ADP and phosphate. This decomposition is exergonic, i.e. spontaneous. The cell now builds catalysts that allow both processes to take place together. In total, the entropy is increased and free energy is destroyed. It can therefore be said that the endergonic build-up of DNA is driven by the exergonic decomposition of ATP.

The same principle is used to create a very high concentration of nutrients within the cell, against the natural gradient. Normally, no glucose molecules would migrate into the cell. However, the cell combines this endergonic process with the influx of sodium ions, which is exergonic. Why is this exergonic? Because the cell previously pumped the sodium out against the equilibrium. Again, this was only possible because this endergonic pumping out was associated with the exergonic decay of ATP. A molecule that is not normally produced, unless it is from the exergonic decomposition of glucose, which is pumped in.

Here you can see that not only occasionally an endergonic reaction is combined with an endergonic reaction and accelerated by a catalyst. There is a whole chain here, even a whole cycle. However, each individual step is exergonic and destroys free energy in the process. This is also the reason why the system must be supplied with energy from outside in order not to come to a standstill.

Of course, the pumps just discussed are not effective in the cell without the cell membrane, which encloses a space. However, both factors together make it possible to generate a very high concentration of nutrients inside the cell. The cell membrane has the task of maintaining these concentrations and preventing the natural balance of concentrations.

The second possibility is based on two processes running in succession. The second process is exergonic and converts the intermediate product produced by the first process into the final product. The first process is endergonic, but it has an equilibrium point where a small part is on the product side. As this product is constantly taken from the second process. process, the first process always has a surplus of reactants and continues to produce exergon.

Both possibilities ensure that endergonic, i.e. non-spontaneous processes can also take place if they are cleverly interconnected and selectively accelerated by catalysts.

9.2   The emergence of order in the organization

The speed of change

Many principles in organizations are based on increasing concentration. This starts with room occupancy, where employees from the same department sit together. Agile principles such as the collocated team or the reduction of work-in-progress also increase concentration. The short distances mean that communication is faster and processes are accelerated.

An alternative to this would be to raise the operating temperature. If everyone is a bit more hectic and walks and talks faster, it would have the same effect. The increased stress makes everything a little more aggressive and there is more energy available. However, this energy doesn't just lead to the creation of structures. Just as much is destroyed.

The energy is necessary, but it must also be targeted. We already know that we need a catalyst for this targeted acceleration.

Catalysis

In organizations, business processes are accelerated when the best working conditions of man, machine, material and method are available. They are the catalyst. This catalyst is also very specific.

The best working conditions ensure that the probability of success in carrying out an activity is significantly increased. The free energy required is reduced.

As a result, many more employees can carry out the process successfully at the first attempt.

However, the best working conditions only help if the employees also want to carry out the process, i.e. the process would otherwise also run spontaneously.

Energetic coupling

We have already seen in the discussion of energetic coupling in the cell that catalysis is the prerequisite for energetic coupling. The catalyst enables a reaction mechanism in which the exergonic and endergonic reactions are combined. The exergonic part drives the overall reaction.

An organization needs a high concentration of success factors, whereby this concentration decreases due to the main theorem. So how can concentrations be increased? Firstly, a system boundary is needed that passively prevents the concentration from being equalized. And it needs active pumps that import the desired factors against the gradient by combining this import with spontaneously occurring processes.

This can also be found in companies. When you hire new employees, you tend to get the average university graduate. But how do you manage to attract the particularly talented ones? It is unlikely that all high potentials will be employed by your company purely by chance. So it is endergon. But if you can offer the prospect of a higher salary, more exciting tasks, more fun and better prospects for the future, it is interesting for applicants. The desire to get a lot of money for a good job is exergon for the applicant. This is combined during the recruitment process. The exergon attracts the endergon process.

Now the question arises as to how the company can afford the high salary. The customer naturally does not want to pay anything (=endergon), unless he receives a high customer benefit (=exergon), so that he has an advantage in total.

The organization achieves the high benefit on the one hand through the high commitment of the new employees and on the other hand through the best possible provision of knowledge and tools. The best working conditions enable high output to be generated without wearing out employees.

However, many employees have no desire to write down their knowledge and pass it on or get rid of bad habits (all endergon), which is why the internal evaluation systems are designed precisely for this purpose. If you want a good evaluation and therefore opportunities for promotion (exergon), you also have to do things that are not so much fun.

All management consultancies have a similar concept. In many cases, catalysts are provided (best working conditions) and endergonic processes are systematically combined with exergonic processes.

So how is order created in an organization? Creating order is not a spontaneous process. Therefore, the creation of order must be combined with spontaneous processes. The driving force is always the spontaneous process.

All of the organization's incentive systems are based on this principle. Unpleasant activities are only carried out if there is something to be gained from them.

9.3 Findings

A **high concentration** of success factors reduces the duration of movements. As a result, all processes run faster. Many lean methods, such as avoiding overproduction with the resulting storage and transportation routes, as well as many agile methods, attempt to increase concentration. However, this high concentration must be created by linking the non-spontaneous increase in concentration with other processes. Concentration must be passively maintained through limits.

Increasing the operating temperature also accelerates processes. However, this destroys just as much as it builds up. Everything goes faster, but not in the right direction.

The third way is closer to the process itself. The best working conditions can be used as a **catalyst** to reduce the need for free energy. This selectively accelerates processes. Less operating temperature is required and less is destroyed.

The **energetic coupling** of processes also allows non-spontaneous processes to take place. A catalyst connects the non-spontaneous process with a spontaneous process so that both run simultaneously. The spontaneous process drives the non-spontaneous process. The energetic coupling can be used to increase concentration or to create structures that are necessary but would never arise spontaneously.

These principles are the abiotic basis on which the bionic organization can then be built. However, the biological principles are of a completely different nature. But that is more the subject of the books Autopoiesis and Cell Culture.

10 Summary

Let's look back at the last few chapters to get an overall picture. Our aim was to lay the physical and chemical foundations for a bionic organizational design. These foundations are intended to explain the mechanisms on which living organisms are based. Important concepts here are energy and entropy.

The many translations and thoughts now provide the foundations for the bionic understanding of organizations, which are described in detail in the books "Autopoiesis" and "Cell Culture".

Let's take a closer look at these principles.

Principle 1: Organizations are inert

An organization continues to move on its current course if no forces act on it. In order to change its direction, or to accelerate or slow down its movement, a force must act on it. The greater the force, the greater the change. However, large organizations require more force for the same change. They have more inertia.

Principle 2: Organizations have energy

Organizations have the energy of movement. This is partly reflected in the change in their key figures. Part of it, the inner energy, is not visible to the outside world and does not contribute to the change in key figures. This inner energy is contained in the many non-value-adding activities that only lead around in circles.

Organizations that want to change are slowed down by difficulties and convert kinetic energy into internal energy. However, some of this energy can be used again.

Principle 3: The only driving force is the increase in entropy

Organizations are complex systems with many possibilities that are constantly changing. From a macroscopic perspective, they always assume the most probable state. Entropy is a measure of the number of possible states or ambiguity. This entropy is constantly increasing.

The driving force of the organization lies in using some of the unused internal energy to change the organization in a targeted manner. To do this, energy must be shifted. However, this is only possible if the overall entropy is increased in the end.

Taking the most probable state is the only power in business! It is not the energy! The increase in entropy is the reason why energy is shifted from one place to another and can thus be harnessed. The energy itself is only an expression of the contained movement of an inherently inert system.

The organization can make clever use of this driving force of entropy by consciously influencing the probability of states.

Principle 4: An isolated organization strives for an equilibrium in which it can no longer change. (second law)

The organization occupies a certain space in the markets. Internally, it has a certain complexity in order to be able to react to the outside world. Maintaining the market position and internal flexibility ties up energy. It only maintains the status quo. The free energy is now the remaining energy. It can be used for new things.

According to the second law of thermodynamics, entropy is constantly increasing. This reduces the free energy (Gibbs energy) to zero.

This means that organizations tend to expand further and further (new products and markets) and increase their internal complexity until it is no longer possible, i.e. the free energy is zero. There is no more energy available for new things. All energy is spent on preservation.

This is the state of equilibrium in which nothing moves.

Principle 5: Organizations must absorb new energy from outside in order to change

Organizations need to import free energy from outside in order to change and continue to grow. This free energy must therefore come from outside, and thus from the stakeholders.

Free energy is not only found in organizations, but also in people. A person who is already busy around the clock no longer has the free energy to create something new for themselves or others.

Principle 6: Non-spontaneous processes can be made to work through energetic coupling.

Moving the organization in the right direction must therefore become more likely than a situation in which everyone does what they want.

The principle is used by linking payment and recognition to the achievement of goals. This link connects the creation of order with a strongly spontaneous process: the desire for money and recognition.

Due to this energetic coupling, non-spontaneous processes also take place, although they seem to contradict the increase in entropy.

Principle 7: Structures must be stable but changeable

Organizations are based on self-generated structures. These must be held together by strong forces so that they remain stable. Nevertheless, it must be possible to change them again.

The principle can be observed in chemistry with atoms and molecules. Molecules must be stable. Only at high energies are the structures destabilized and chemical reactions take place that transform the molecules.

In the same way, working environments in the organization must be reliable and stable. However, it must also be possible to change them.

Principle 8: The speed of processes depends on the operating temperature.

The speed of processes depends on the operating temperature. In organizations, the temperature is the average energy expended per target. If there are too many targets, the energy is distributed over too many degrees of freedom, so that too little energy is available for a particular target.

Whenever new degrees of freedom are added, the temperature stagnates. For this reason, it is found that an organization does not generate more output despite increased resources. This principle also explains the Mythical Man-Month. 10 people do not necessarily achieve twice as much as 5 people, even if they are all hard-working. Their energy is often lost in an increased number of internal degrees of freedom.

Principle 9: The speed of processes depends on the concentration.

The speed of processes depends on concentration. High specialization and short distances ensure high productivity.

Principle 10: The speed of processes can be increased by catalysts.

The best working conditions change the flow of a process in such a way that less free energy is required from employees. The process is therefore simpler and can be carried out by many more employees with considerably less energy. This results in shorter waiting times.

This follows directly from the Maxwell-Boltzmann distribution, which - translated to organizations - states that high energy values can only be found in a small number of employees. Lowering the required free energy significantly increases the number of possible candidates.

Conclusion:

Viewing organizations from the perspective of physics and chemistry provides a new perspective. It shows the abiotic foundations of a bionic organization.

I hope the book has given you some new inspiration. If you enjoyed it, I would be delighted if you would recommend it, write a review or send me your feedback directly.

Live long and prosper,

Clemens Dachs

11 Bibliography

Alberts, B., Johnson, A., Lewis, J., Raff, M., David, M., Roberts, K., & Walter, P. (2015). *Molecularbiology of the cell, 6thEdition.* Abingdon: Garland Science.

Atkins, P. (2017). *Four Laws of the Universe.* Oxford Un versity Press.

Atkins, P., Paula, J. d., & Keeler, J. (2018). *Physical Chemistry.* Oxford: Oxford University Press.

Bartelmann, M., Feuerbacher, B., Krüger, T., Lüst, D., Rebhan, A. K., & Wipf, A. (2018). *Theoretische Physik 1.* Berlin, Heidelberg: Springer Spektrum.

Dachs, C. (2021). *Viable Project Business.* Heidelberg: Soringer.

Dachs, C. (2022). *Autopoiesis.* Norderstedt: Book on Demand.

Dachs, C., & Hornung, M. (2021). *Zellkultur.* Vachendorf: Nova MD .

Frahm, M., & Roll, C. (1022). *Designing Intelligent Construction Projects.* Wiley-Blackwell.

Lambertz, M. (2021). *Die intelligente Organisation.* Business Village.

Nolting, W. (2018). *Grundkurs Theoretische Physik 1 - Klassische Mechanik und mathematische Vorbereitungen.* Berlin, Heidelberg: Springer Spektrum.

Schiller, F., & Heider, M. (2021). *SCRUM Master Kompagnon.* dpunkt Verlag.

Sisney, L. (2012). *Organizational Physics.* Lula.

Willkomm, D. (2021). *Roadmap durch die VUCA-Welt.* UVK Verlag.